Lives of Service

Guided only by her sense of touch, a blind massage therapist works inside the Maryknoll-sponsored Seeing Eyes clinic in Phnom Penh, the first program for the blind in Cambodia.

Lives of Service

Stories from Maryknoll

Photographs and Text by Jim Daniels

ORBIS BOOKS

Maryknoll, New York 10545

for Mary Lello
partner, accomplice, healer and friend

The Catholic Foreign Mission Society of America (Maryknoll) recruits and trains people for overseas missionary service. Through Orbis Books, Maryknoll aims to foster the international dialogue that is essential to mission.

To obtain more information about Maryknoll and Orbis Books, please visit our website at www.maryknoll.org

Library of Congress Cataloging-in-Publication Data is available upon request.

ISBN 1-57075-308-3

To find out more about Maryknoll, contact:

Maryknoll Sisters
P. O. Box 311
Maryknoll, NY 10545-0311

Phone: 914-941-7575
Fax: 914-923-0733
E-Mail: hphillips@mksisters.org

Maryknoll Fathers & Brothers
P. O. Box 304
Maryknoll, NY 10545-0304

Phone: 914-941-7590
Fax: 914-941-0735
E-Mail: mkweb@maryknoll.org

Maryknoll Mission Association of the
Faithful
P.O. Box 307
Maryknoll, NY 10545-0307

Phone: 914-762-6364
Toll Free: 800-818-5276
Fax: 914-762-7031
E-Mail: mmaf@mkl-mmaf.org

Maryknoll Affiliates
3600 S. Seeley Ave.
Chicago, IL 60609-1148

Phone: 773-927-9257
E-Mail: inquiry@maryknollaffiliates.org

Contents

For a photojournalist, finding Maryknoll was something like an archaeologist discovering the Lost City of the Incas; an abundance of remarkable stories lay about me waiting to be uncovered. Here were hundreds of women and men, united by their faith and commitment, serving humanity in remote corners of the world, and I had the good fortune to be asked to gather a few of these stories. For over four years, I travelled to remote parts of the globe where I met inspiring people who allowed me into their lives. The journey was remarkable.

Just getting to some of these locations was an exercise in faith. Vince Cole lives in a remote jungle village in West Papua (Irian Jaya), three hours up-river from the grass strip where the bush plane lands. Six months before my visit, Vince and I had talked on the phone while he was on his once-every-five-year visit to Maryknoll. "Yeah, come when you want," he had said casually. "I'll probably be there." As I headed up-river in a small boat, through dense smoke on the Pomat River, passing naked families in dugout canoes, I realized that I was in the same area where David Rockefeller's son disappeared back in the 1960s, presumably killed by Asmat head-hunters. When the boat finally landed in the tiny village, I was more than a little relieved to see a smiling Vince Cole standing on his dock in cut-off blue jeans.

In order to see Dr. Susan Nagele's work at the health clinic in the Sudan, we had to convoy along a dangerous road from Lokichokio, Kenya to Narus, Sudan, where on the previous day snipers had fired automatic weapons at passing cars. In the village, a decomposed body lay on the side of a hill, a few feet from hundreds of spent AK-47 shell casings. We returned to Kenya along the same road one night, approaching each rebel checkpoint with car lights flashing and my heart pounding. In between, I learned how this soft-spoken woman survived for seven years in a war zone — with grace and compassion.

Although I was with these people for only a little while, the time was compressed and often intense. From shopping at a bazaar with Bob McCahill in Bangladesh, to riding in the back of a truck in Burma with John Beeching, to walking through a poor neighborhood in Phnom Penh with Juana Encalada, there was always an opportunity to learn. These Maryknollers, and the people they share their lives with, became my teachers. I learned to open my eyes and my heart to the world. And always there were unexpected gifts.

Late one night, as Susan Nagele and I sat under a bright African sky, shots rang out. This was immediately followed by loud singing and laughter. I felt compelled to check it out. At first Susan refused but eventually relented and along with others we walked into the bush. There we found twenty young men standing in a circle singing as one man in the middle jumped to the rhythm. I watched transfixed until one of the men grabbed me by the arm and pulled me into the circle. There, under a full Toposa moon, jumping and laughing like a madman in a place better known for war, I found the metaphor for my life's work: To witness and participate in another's life, and to lose and find a little of myself along the way.

The World
of Maryknoll

The model for the spirit of service can be found in the loving
relationship between a mother and child. Here, a
Toposa woman in the Sudan, carries her child on her back.

MARYKNOLL is the popular name of a Catholic family of nearly fourteen hundred priests, sisters, brothers, and lay missioners working in service among the poor and faithful in over thirty countries across the globe. With the Gospel as their guide, the U.S.-based Maryknoll missioners leave the relative security of their own homes in order to discover God in the faces of their neighbors in "fields afar." Convinced of the scriptural teaching that we cannot claim to know and love God if we have not known and loved others, the Maryknollers can be found living among marginalized communities in Asia, Africa, Latin America, the Pacific, and the Middle East. There they join not only their fellow Catholics but also people of different religious and cultural traditions in an effort to build a world of justice, peace, and understanding. At times they bear witness through words or deeds. At times, they work in silence.

There are three distinct organizations within the Maryknoll family: the Catholic Foreign Mission Society of America (the Maryknoll Fathers and Brothers); the Maryknoll Sisters of St. Dominic (better known simply as the Maryknoll Sisters); and the Maryknoll Mission Association of the Faithful (predominantly lay people, both individuals and families, though it is also open to clergy and religious of other orders). While each group is an independent entity with its own governing body, they are all brought together, under the Maryknoll name, to commit their lives to Christ through witness, prayer, and service. While answering Christ's call to live and proclaim the Gospel, Maryknollers maintain a deep and authentic respect for other religious traditions; their mission is a matter of active witness, not simply focused on conversion.

For many people around the globe the name of Maryknoll is particularly associated with the defense of human rights and social justice, often within countries where oppression is the rule and such a stance entails considerable risk. This commitment was powerfully dramatized in our lifetime by the death of two Maryknoll Sisters (along with two other North American church-women) who were brutally murdered by the Salvadoran military in 1980. But the commitment to justice and human welfare is equally visible in the work of those Maryknollers, the majority, whose efforts are not shadowed by persecution.

The Maryknoll Seminary building in Ossining, New York.

Maryknoll Sisters in Tanzania, 1942.

A procession in Tanzania, one of Maryknoll's earliest missions in Africa.

Father James A. Walsh, co-founder of Maryknoll, with Chinese children.

Crowds assemble at St. Peter's Basilica during the Second Vatican Council.

As an organization with ninety years of history, Maryknoll has seen its mission evolve in response to the developing needs of those it serves as well as to the enormous changes in both the church and the world. At the time of Maryknoll's first mission in 1918, when four American priests traveled to Yeungkong, China, the United States had only recently been removed from the Vatican's list of mission territories. Aware of the historic nature of their new mission to China, the early Maryknoll missioners were drawn by the exciting possibility of developing the Church and spreading the Gospel in foreign lands. While working to nourish the local church, the Maryknoll mission always entailed efforts to relieve the suffering of the sick and the poor.

In China, for example, Maryknoll helped establish schools, nutrition centers, leper colonies, and health care centers. Meanwhile, the missioners faced a variety of hardships, including illness and harsh living conditions, and ultimately the reality of outright persecution. Pressures came first from a Chinese government wary of foreign interference, then later from the occupying Japanese, who saw the missioners as enemy agents, and finally from the Communists who came to power after World War II and who eventually banned Maryknoll from the country.

In other lands and other places Maryknoll carried on the work of proclamation and service. But in religious terms there are significant differences between the motivation of Maryknoll's early missioners and those of today. Mission in the early part of the twentieth century, as in previous history, was strongly characterized by an emphasis on "saving souls" and a triumphalistic extension of Catholic "territory."

Years later at Vatican II (1962-65), Catholic teaching evolved in significant ways. The mission of the church is not simply to extend its own borders but to serve God's Kingdom, and to bear witness to the love of God revealed in Jesus Christ. This perspective opened up new dimensions for the mission of Maryknoll. Along with ongoing humanitarian service Maryknollers also became involved in projects to empower the poor and to affirm their basic human dignity. Along with proclamation of the Gospel, Maryknollers became increasingly drawn to seek out the face of God in the diverse cultures and religious traditions of other peoples.

Along with theological changes, political events of the world have also shaped Maryknoll's mission in fundamental ways. In China, the Japanese occupation during World War II and the subsequent Communist revolution were times of systematic harassment and persecution. Many Maryknollers were arrested and imprisoned under harsh conditions. Eventually the Maryknollers, along with all foreign missionaries, were expelled from China. But while this closed one mission field it opened the door to others, particularly in Latin America and later in other parts of Asia, Africa, and the Pacific.

In 1942 Maryknoll established a mission in Bolivia, the beginning of what would become an extensive presence in Latin America. Unlike in China, the people of these countries were almost entirely Catholic, yet, due to the insufficient number of clergy, their experience of the church was often remote and confined to baptisms and other special occasions. In this context the work of Maryknoll focused on building the local church through religious education, the formation of community, and the training of lay pastoral leaders. The aim of the Maryknollers was to foster a sense of human dignity and a consciousness among the poor of their value as children of God. At the same time, most of the countries in Latin America had a long history of oppressive governance by powerful oligarchies whose rule was often maintained by brutal force. Efforts to promote social justice were regularly suppressed with terrifying violence. In such a situation those who stood beside the oppressed and joined their cry for justice—even priests and nuns—were subject to the same fate.

With Vatican II the church entered a new era of open commitment to peace and social justice. By 1971 the world's bishops had declared that the pursuit of justice was a "constitutive" part of proclaiming the Gospel. In similar terms the bishops in Latin America spoke of the church's "preferential option for the poor." Maryknollers were among those who took this challenge to heart. In 1980 the horrific murder of four North American church-women, including Maryknoll Sisters Maura Clarke and Ita Ford, by a military death squad in El Salvador dramatized to the world the powerful commitment represented by this option and the terrible price some would have to pay.

Nuns pray over the disinterred bodies of the four churchwomen, including Maryknoll Sisters Ita Ford and Maura Clarke, slain in El Salvador in December 1980.

Father James A. Walsh, co-founder of Maryknoll, in the early office of The Field Afar.

THE GENESIS OF MARYKNOLL came in a hotel lobby in Montreal in 1910. Two American priests, Father Thomas Price and Father James Anthony Walsh, sat down together and discussed their converging ideas of creating a mission society in America. The founders of Maryknoll had very different backgrounds. Thomas Price grew up in Wilmington, North Carolina, the son of Catholic converts, while James Anthony Walsh was a first-generation Irish-American from Boston.

Price, the first ordained Catholic priest in North Carolina, had spent almost twenty years walking the backwoods of his predominantly Protestant state preaching the Gospel. Called "the Tar Heel Apostle," he is widely credited with establishing the Catholic church in North Carolina. Price was, by all accounts, a tireless and extremely enthusiastic man whose dedication to his faith was intense and unflappable. He was deeply devoted to Mary, the Blessed Mother (whom he credited with saving him from drowning during a shipwreck while on his way to the seminary), and he wrote her letters daily. A dreamer and mystic, he was in many ways the opposite of his eventual partner, Father Walsh.

James Anthony Walsh, the son of Irish immigrants, was born in Cambridge, Massachusetts, educated at Boston College, and later at Harvard University. Having discovered his call to the priesthood while at Harvard, he quickly transferred to St. John's Seminary outside Boston, where he was ordained a priest in 1892. It was at the seminary that the young Walsh learned about the church "outside of Boston" and became fascinated by the idea of foreign mission. In 1903 Walsh was appointed diocesan director of the Society for the Propagation of the Faith and took over control of its Boston office. Four years later he founded *The Field Afar*, a magazine about foreign missions of the Catholic church. It was in this period that his dream of establishing an American mission society began to take root. Father Walsh began to discuss the idea openly with his peers but it was his chance encounter with Father Price at the Ecumenical Congress in Montreal that set Maryknoll's future in motion.

Father Thomas Price, co-founder of Maryknoll, with three of the original Maryknoll Fathers. These include, on his right, Father James E. Walsh, who later spent twelve years as a prisoner of the Chinese Communists, and Father Francis X. Ford, on his left, who died in a Chinese prison.

After their Montreal meeting, Price and Walsh wrote each other frequently, discussing their vision and plans for its implementation. During these initial talks it became apparent that they held strongly divergent views on the focus of their new society, whether it should be dedicated exclusively to foreign mission or some combination of home and foreign mission. Price, reflecting his experience in the South, embraced the latter, while Walsh was adamant about the former. Eventually Price acquiesced, and the focus of their new organization was firmly fixed on mission overseas. After receiving the approval of the American bishops in 1911, they took their proposal to Rome. With the blessing of Pope Pius X the new society became a reality. So was born the Catholic Foreign Mission Society of America.

The origins of the Maryknoll Sisters lie with a young woman named Mary Josephine ("Mollie") Rogers, the daughter of a prosperous Irish-American family from Jamaica Plain, Massachusetts. While studying at Smith College, Rogers was deeply inspired by the example of fellow students—Protestants—who were then signing a pledge to teach in mission schools in China. She regretted that at that time there were no similar programs available to Catholic students at the college. After her graduation, when Rogers returned to Smith as an instructor, she was given the opportunity to start a mission club for Smith's Catholic students. These efforts eventually led her to the Boston office of Father James Anthony Walsh, who had recently begun publishing his fledgling mission publication. As two Boston Irish Catholics with a keen interest in foreign mission, Walsh and Rogers recognized an immediate bond. Soon Rogers began volunteering on *The Field Afar*, the journal which, many years later, would become known as *Maryknoll* magazine.

In 1911 Fathers Walsh and Price were making plans to establish a new seminary for training American young men for foreign mission. This would become the home of the new Catholic Foreign Mission Society of America. A parcel of land was ultimately found north of New York City in Westchester County on a hilltop overlooking the Hudson River. The new site was named after Mary, leading to the name by which the society is known to this day: Maryknoll.

Mollie Rogers had been working full time for Walsh when the priest invited her, along with three other young women, to join the new society and move to New York. They all accepted and Rogers was finally able to join the group in 1912. While the priests' vision for this new society was always intended for men, Rogers had never forgotten the inspiration she received years earlier at Smith and she dreamed of establishing an American religious mission community for women.

Mary Josephine (Mollie) Rogers before she went to work for Father Walsh.

Mother Mary Joseph Rogers, founder of the Maryknoll Sisters.

Maryknoll Sister Celine Marie, one of the early missioners in China.

On Valentine's Day of 1920 the Vatican officially recognized the Maryknoll Sisters, and Rogers, now called by her religious name, Mother Mary Joseph, became the first superior. There were thirty-five women in the original group and the following year six of them left for China. Mother Mary Joseph felt strongly that the Sisters should adapt to their surroundings, learning the language and customs of their new Chinese neighbors. "If there is any conversion," she observed, "we are the ones who should change."

This principle of cultural sensitivity has become one of the hallmarks of all Maryknoll missions. Rather than go abroad as representatives of the United States or the West, Maryknollers are engaged in a quest to find God's presence within the myriad cultures of the world. In that process Maryknollers identify with, and share in, the daily struggles of their neighbors. And through this interaction with people of other faiths and cultures they experience a deepening of their own Catholic faith.

Although for Maryknoll, as for other religious communities in recent years, vocations to the priesthood and religious life are lower than in the past, the Maryknoll family has widened to incorporate other forms of mission life. Once again the influence of Vatican II was felt within Maryknoll in the late 1970s with the growing recognition of the role of laity within the church. In 1975 a lay mission program was formed within Maryknoll that invited single men and women, couples, and families to join as partners in Maryknoll's mission outreach. Since that time, over four hundred lay people have responded passionately to the mission call, serving as doctors, nurses, teachers, lawyers, social workers, and pastoral agents in many countries overseas.

In 1994 Maryknoll's lay mission program evolved into the Maryknoll Mission Association of the Faithful (MMAF) in recognition of the ability of laity to respond to the church's global mission. The Maryknoll Mission Association has shown steady growth since its inception and now has members serving in fourteen countries around the world. Maryknoll's lay missioners hail from many different parts of the United States and represent a wide range of ages, skills, and interests. All share the common goal of living a life of Christian service to the poor.

For lay people who desire to participate in mission but find it difficult to commit to a three-year assignment, Maryknoll has established a program of Maryknoll Affiliates for foreign mission. While many Affiliates remain in the United States promoting the work of Maryknoll in their home regions, others travel abroad as short-term volunteers, assisting Maryknollers as needs arise. Many participants are attracted to mission through their desire to be of service to the world and to elevate their travel experiences to a spiritual level. As with MMAF, the Affiliate program has seen a regular increase in the numbers of participants.

Maryknoll lay missioners in 1977.

Maryknoll Father Joseph Hanh with parishioners in Bolivia, in the 1940s.

Maryknoll Father Frank Breen in Kenya.

Maryknoll Father William McCarthy with a base community in Peru, in the 1980s.

THE WORK OF MARYKNOLL is as varied as it is widespread. Maryknollers have backgrounds in medicine, education, communications, and spiritual formation. They come from families of wealth and of poverty. The lives featured in the following chapters are simply a sampler of the wider Maryknoll movement, seven examples that were culled from the scores of Maryknoll missions currently in place around the world. The scores of mission projects not mentioned in this book continue today in relative anonymity and are no less important: places such as Lima, Peru, where a Maryknoll priest is helping to protect the human rights of street children, or in the Philippines, where Maryknoll Sisters are counseling families in crisis, or in Vietnam, where a married couple is providing skills training to the poor of Hanoi. There are Maryknollers assisting the people of Venezuela rebuild their lives after floods washed their dreams away. At the same moment lay missioners are digging wells in the Peruvian Andes so that accessible fresh water is no longer only a dream.

These stories are meant as a celebration. They are intended to honor the spirit of Maryknoll, including the hundreds of men and women of Maryknoll and the unique communities with whom they share their lives. Each village, hamlet, and neighborhood represents a host of challenges and a unique opportunity for faith and understanding. The difficulties faced by the people these Maryknollers support can at times be overwhelming. In every case, however, Maryknollers have managed to discover God in the faces of the people.

New Maryknoll missioners at their departure ceremony in 1993.

John Beeching, a Maryknoll Brother working in Thailand, talks about holding "the body of Christ" as an indigent man dies in his arms. Bob McCahill, a Maryknoll priest in Bangladesh, talks of the "compassion of Allah" as he witnesses brilliant generosity in his destitute Muslim neighbors. Susan Nagele, a lay missioner and physician, finds "miracles" in her medical work in an impoverished war zone in Sudan that make it difficult for her to imagine returning home. Sister Juana Encalada describes her work among HIV/AIDS patients in Cambodia as an effort to "witness to the presence of God in their lives." After living sixteen years in the remote Indonesian village of Sa-Er, tears come to the eyes of Maryknoll priest Vince Cole as he recalls how a neighbor named his first-born after him. Peter and Johanna Kailing, lay missioners in Kenya, describe receiving lessons in friendship and gratitude. Melinda Roper, a Maryknoll Sister in Panama, describes what it means to accompany the people in mission: "We discover the beauty and tragedy of life together."

These are simple tales of faith and love where people from different backgrounds have discovered a common humanity and have forged enduring friendships. These are stories, like many others, that deserve to be told. They are all stories of communion and hope for the twenty-first century.

JIM DANIELS

Maryknoll Brother Andy Massalek in Mexico.

Lay missioner Fred Goddard in the Philippines.

In the Arms of Allah

"I'm not interested in them becoming Christians.
I want them to be the best Muslims they can be.
One who serves the poor serves Allah."

— *Father Bob McCahill*

*Mojid Ali, a young Muslim man suffering from cancer and too weak to walk,
stares back over Bob McCahill's shoulder as he's carried down a long
walkway at the hospital in Mymensingh, Bangladesh. He was taken to an
overly crowded ward with no available beds; he was given space on the floor.*

1 *A crowd of people looking for food gathers just outside the main door of the Missionaries of Charity's center in Dhaka, Bangladesh. McCahill went to visit a child at the center's orphanage where the organization, made famous by its founder, Mother Teresa, cares for abandoned children.*

2 *McCahill's preferred mode of transit is a Chinese bike. He says that the bike has become a symbol of his commitment to the people. "They see you are serious in the exertion of love."*

1

THE HOSPITAL AT MYMENSINGH, much like the rest of Bangladesh, is bursting at the seams. The narrow corridors of this sprawling facility are jammed with hundreds of people standing in line outside the dimly lit doctor's offices or moving from room to room seeking relatives in one of the overcrowded wards. On a long wooden bench near the front entrance, a frail man dressed in a traditional print skirt sits with his eyes closed.

Maryknoll Father Bob McCahill, known locally as Brother Bob, walks over to the man, whom he had promised to meet. The missioner lifts the man into his arms and quickly joins the river of people flowing into the hospital. Mojid Ali, a Muslim man in his twenties, is suffering from advanced cancer. Too weak to walk, he stares back over McCahill's shoulder with a look of both resignation and fear as they make their way down a long walkway. For more than fifteen minutes McCahill carries Ali, down four corridors, up three long flights of stairs, until he finally arrives at the packed ward where Ali has been assigned. Every single bed and most of the floor space is already taken up with the sick and dying. An overworked and visibly stressed nurse points to a patch of open floor. A thin bamboo mat is spread, and McCahill gently lays Ali down.

The hospital in Mymensingh is a two-hour bus ride along a narrow highway from McCahill's home in Sherpur, three hours from the capital of Dhaka. In a country roughly the size of Maine, there are over one hundred twenty million souls in Bangladesh, making it the most densely populated country on the planet. As one would expect, the rising tide of humanity has flooded the land with brutal poverty.

2

McCahill, who has nursing training, had met Mojid Ali much as he does the other patients he helps, by riding through the countryside on his Chinese-made bicycle searching out the sick and disabled. In Ali's case, McCahill was approached by a relative who had heard of the missioner's service to the sick and brought the Maryknoller to Ali's home. After seeing that he warranted medical attention, McCahill provided bus fare to Mymensingh as well as notes written in flowing Bengali Sanskrit to be read by bus drivers and hospital staff along the way. In addition, McCahill provided some money for food and medicine along with a promise to meet Ali at the hospital the following Wednesday. This was all standard procedure for Bob McCahill's unique mission.

Bob McCahill grew up in Goshen, Indiana, and received his call to ministry in "a moment of ecstasy" when he was a teenager. Entering Maryknoll, he was ordained as a priest in 1964. While working in the Philippines, his first Maryknoll mission, he heard about a terrible tidal wave in Bangladesh that killed hundreds of thousands of people. News of that tragedy, as well as the ongoing starvation that was killing a million more, rocked McCahill to the point where he thought, "There must be something I can do." He eventually applied for a transfer and arrived in Bangladesh in 1975. He began assisting the sick poor, helping ill and disabled people to receive medical attention and Christian love. His intention from the outset was to live as close to his poor Muslim neighbors as possible and "simply show them that we are one."

In a society where the population is roughly 88 percent Muslim and 11 percent Hindu, Christians are nearly non-existent, making up less than one half of one percent. There is a natural mistrust by many Bangladeshis of people of other faiths. This is especially true of Christian missionaries, whose motive, they assume, is to lure them from Islam. According to McCahill, many missionaries have indeed cloaked their agenda of conversion behind offers of help. As for himself, he is determined never to exploit his neighbors' poverty "as a way to insert the Gospel message."

During his twenty-four years in Bangladesh, McCahill has chosen to live in rural towns, staying no more than three years in any one place before moving on to another village. His decision to relocate frequently comes from a strong desire to practice what he calls "basic Christianity," recalling the example of Jesus who traveled from village to village, living among the poor. He also wants to avoid creating financial or emotional dependency on the part of the community he serves. His emphasis is on following the example of Christ and not, as he puts it, "being an administrator of funds." Although he shares the same conditions and poverty as his neighbors—living in a tiny hut with no electricity or running water—he does often pay some medical bills for the sick people he assists. But it is vital for McCahill that people not perceive a connection between his Christian service and money, as this would undermine his essential mission. He simply wants to live a life of unconditional love.

He recalls the time a man arrived at his door, asking to become a Christian. "Really?" the missioner replied incredulously. "Now why would you want to do that?" The man replied that he had heard that if he were to convert he would receive money from the church. All of the Christians he knew were rich, he said. "Have you studied your own religion?" the Maryknoller asked. McCahill suggested that he turn to his own faith more deeply and put his trust in Allah. The man did not ask again.

1

1 Downtown Dhaka is the chaotic, noisy capital of the most densely populated country in the world.

2 During a visit to a small town, villagers who had implored the priest to show them a photograph of his American parents surround Bob McCahill.

3 A group of women use long rakes as they turn lentils drying in the sun in Sherpur, Bangladesh.

2

3

McCahill observes that during the three years that he lives in each village his evolving relationship with the community has a pattern. The first year he lives in a new place he is usually met with suspicion. Here he is a man living alone with no wife or family—and a Christian, as well. But slowly the people become more used to seeing him coming and going on his bike and helping people and by the second year there is a growing sense of trust. "The bike is key," McCahill says. "They see me riding around, working my rear end off for other people. This impresses them. They see you are serious in the exertion of love." Charity and kindness are revered traits in Islamic society and Allah is often referred to as "the Compassionate One." This is a point McCahill at times makes with his Muslim acquaintances when they challenge the priest about his Christian beliefs.

By the third year real affection has taken root. "Bengalis don't give a lot of feedback," McCahill reflects with a laugh. "This isn't a praise society." But his acceptance as a neighbor is evidenced by frequent calls of "Hello, Brother Bob!" from people greeting him as he walks through the bazaar to buy the day's meal of vegetables and eggs. People come up to him frequently just to say hello or appear at his door to ask for help with a sick relative. His mission is one of utter service to the poor with no interest in converting his neighbors to Christianity. In fact, during his years in Bangladesh, McCahill has always kept his own devotional life a very personal matter. However, when asked, as he frequently is, who he is and why he does what he does, McCahill candidly responds, "I am your Christian brother. I go about doing good and healing because that is what Jesus did. Jesus is my model; I am his follower."

A woman walks alongside an expansive wheat field on the outskirts of Sherpur. Women do much of the farming labor in Bangladesh.

1 *At the bazaar in the town of Sherpur, a man sells colorful powders used in Hindu religious ceremonies.*

2 *Two young girls stay close to their mother inside a tiny village on the outskirts of Jamalpur.*

3 *A man tends his rice crop in his field outside of Sherpur. Rice and lentils are staples of the Bengali diet.*

4 *The roads of Bangladesh are always full of people, many of whom just stand off the side and watch the world, such as these three.*

3

4

An hour before the first call to prayer lifts from the mosque across the street, McCahill rises to meditate for an hour and then to celebrate Mass alone in the pre-dawn darkness. Sitting cross-legged on the packed dirt of his tiny hut and illuminated only by the weak light of his oil lamp, McCahill consecrates the Eucharist as his Muslim neighbors sleep in their homes a few feet away.

Once Mass has ended and the brightening sky appears through the cracks in the bamboo walls, the interior of his modest cabin comes into view. Water for coffee steams away on a small kerosene burner suspended on three bricks on the floor. On one wall two old spoons are wedged behind a narrow bamboo strip, and a large metal urn holding water from the tube-well rests on the earth next to an old trunk with a rusting lock. When the bedding is rolled up, the raised wooden platform doubles as a table. Above the platform, a box of papers and a few books make up the library. Some clothes hang on a line stretched from corner to corner. All appear to be artifacts of a life that is utterly simple, ordered, and efficient.

Just as he begins to pour his first cup of coffee, the silence is transformed by the haunting voice of the imam rising in a steady crescendo above Sherpur, calling all to praise Allah.

There is a natural curiosity between the Christian priest and his Muslim neighbors that works both ways. Once McCahill went to the local mosque to pray and to observe and was welcomed until a member of the congregation approached the imam to object, saying that the presence of a Christian disturbed him. Later, McCahill and the man spoke about this pervasive fear that Christians are interested only in snaring converts. The priest asked, "Why would it be necessary for all of us to be of the same religion in order to be close to one another? Are you afraid of me and I of you? I don't want anything for you that you don't want for yourself."

Dawn is still an hour away as McCahill prepares to celebrate Mass by lantern light inside his tiny hut in the village of Sherpur. The priest chooses this time of day so as not to offend his Muslim neighbors.

1

1 *A young Bangladeshi girl walks by the side of the road.*
The tilaka, a vermilion-colored red spot on her forehead,
signifies that she is a follower of the Hindu religion.

2 *A woman takes a break from drying lentils in the blazing,*
mid-day sun to pour a bucket of water over her head.

3 *McCahill stops on his ride back home to check the progress*
of a boy who is fighting an illness.

2

Aside from Jesus, Bob McCahill draws particular inspiration from the example of Mahatma Gandhi, who renounced all luxury in his selfless service of the poor. Though Gandhi remained committed to the Hinduism of his birth, he wrote a set of challenging reflections on Christianity, *The Message of Jesus Christ,* that had a profound impact on McCahill's own understanding of the Gospel and his view of mission. McCahill says that Gandhi's teachings helped shape his appreciation of other faiths, such as Islam, and the wisdom of totally accepting whatever faith one is called to. For the Maryknoll priest the link between faiths is love or, more specifically, "disinterested love," meaning the love that asks for nothing in return. It is this ideal of pure altruism—the true Christian model that is beyond the need to persuade or proselytize—that fires McCahill's passion. And it seems to strike a chord of wonder in his Muslim neighbors, who are astonished by such acts of genuine kindness by someone of a different faith. He overheard one Muslim man confide to a friend, "This man practices Islam better than we do!"

3

FROM ALL DIRECTIONS the sounds of the awakening village rush through the paper-thin walls of McCahill's home. Women gathering at the community tube-well just a few feet from the missioner's dwelling can be heard filling their tin containers with water and greeting each other in loud voices. The sound of cascading water mixes with the squeals of laughing children. Meanwhile another neighbor, a rickshaw driver, shouts to his wife as he rides off to the center of town in search of fares. Bengali music, playing on a battery-operated radio, suddenly blasts from the house behind the stove.

A little before seven, McCahill emerges through the small opening of his hut, mounts his bike, and starts another day riding through the countryside. He pedals his Phoenix bike along the hot, crowded road to Jamalpur, passing through tiny villages that sprout up between the rice fields like tufts of humanity floating in a sea of green. Overcrowded buses thunder by on the narrow road at terrific speeds, their human cargo hanging out of windows and totally covering the roof. McCahill, dressed in khaki slacks, slippers, and a woven bag slung over his shoulder, rides at a fast pace, expertly maneuvering his bike through vehicles, people, and herds of cattle. An hour and a half later he arrives at the ferry for the ten-minute ride across the Brahmaputra River to Jamalpur.

Once in town McCahill weaves his way quickly through the press of cars and rick-shaws until he turns off the main road onto a dirt path leading to a small village near a stand of trees. There he finds Samidul Islam lying on a mat outside his home. Samidul has advanced cancer and, knowing his time is short, has asked to be taken outside to give his family more room in their tiny house.

Bob McCahill speaks to the man in a comforting voice. His wife produces a battered and folded x-ray, too old to be of any use, but McCahill looks at it anyway and offers to buy some medicine for Samidul. As he leaves to return to Sherpur, a visitor asks whether he finds it depressing to minister to the dying. The Maryknoller simply replies, "I'm not called to succeed. I'm called to help."

McCahill pays a visit to a dying man who lies on a mat outside his home. In severely crowded Bangladesh, the dying will often be moved outside to make more room for family members in their tiny homes. The x-ray is battered and too old to be medically useful yet the man asks McCahill to look at it.

Seedling of Hope

"I don't like to say that I am here to help.
That sounds like I am above them.
It's about sharing, mutual respect, and learning."

— *Sister Juana Encalada*

Inside a clinic outside the capital, Juana Encalada greets a woman with AIDS whom the Maryknoll nun has been assisting in finding treatment and offering emotional support.

A LITTLE AFTER EIGHT ONE MORNING, Maryknoll Sister Juana Encalada dons her white motorcycle helmet and sunglasses. She steps out from a health care and educational center on a busy boulevard in downtown Phnom Penh, capital of Cambodia. Behind the diminutive Peruvian woman, a sign in English, Khmer, and Vietnamese reads: "Seedling of Hope, A Maryknoll Project."

On the wide street, a horde of mopeds along with trucks, cars, and even an odd oxcart choke the air with noise and dust. In the crowd of pedestrians hurrying along the sidewalk, many, with colorful scarves around their faces to protect against the airborne dirt, look like Bedouins in the desert. A loudspeaker blares Buddhist prayers from a temple on the corner.

In Khmer, Encalada quietly negotiates the fare with a moped taxi driver. She climbs sidesaddle onto the vehicle, and they meld into the traffic for the short ride to the hospital where she is scheduled to visit a young woman dying of AIDS. It's the start of a typical day for the Maryknoll missioner.

1

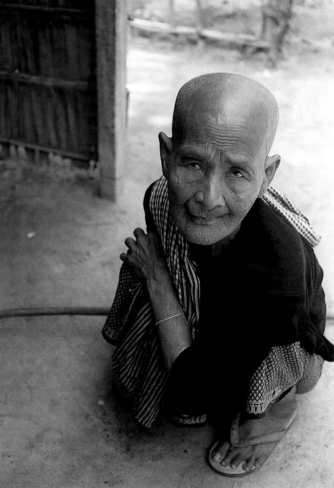
2

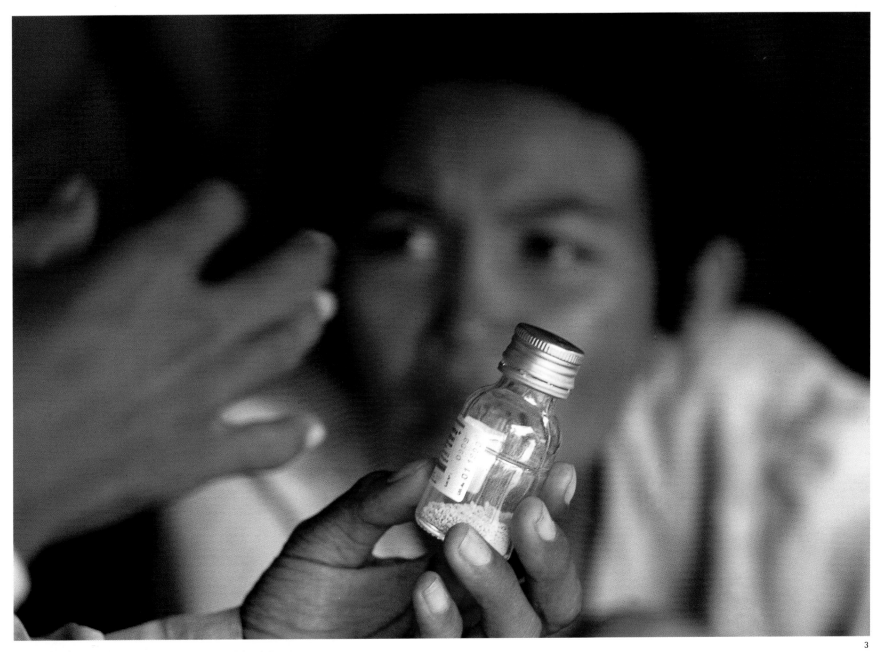

1 *Cambodians leave the countryside and come to Phnom Penh looking for work and a chance at a better life.*

2 *In a small village on the outskirts of the capital, an elderly woman visits a neighbor who is living with AIDS.*

3 *A woman suffering with AIDS listens as a doctor explains to her the scores of medications she must take.*

4 *A detail showing a Hindu deity from a panel on an outside wall of one of the ancient temples at Angkor Wat in Siem Reap, Cambodia.*

4

1

1 *A young boy plays with a toy gun near a house in a poor village outside Phnom Penh.*

2 *Inside a private clinic in Phnom Penh, a victim of a land mine sleeps in one of the wards. The millions of land mines and unexploded ordnance that are littered throughout the Cambodian countryside have made people with missing limbs a familiar sight.*

3 *Inside the Killing Fields Memorial outside Phnom Penh, hundreds of skulls are stacked inside a display just a few yards from the hundreds of graves where the Khmer Rouge crudely buried their victims. Over two million Cambodians were murdered during their reign.*

2

Twenty years after the end of the notorious Pol Pot era, Cambodia remains a country in shock, still reeling from the events that began on April 17, 1975. On that day, following five years of a brutal war and years of American bombing, the Khmer Rouge triumphantly marched into the capital of Phnom Penh and abruptly proceeded to tear down all facets of society. It was the beginning of one of history's most sweeping and brutal experiments in social revolution. The Khmer Rouge emptied the entire city of Phnom Penh, driving the population into the countryside to become peasants for the revolution. People who spoke another language or were of a higher education—even people who wore eyeglasses— became counter-revolutionary suspects and were often shot on the spot. The dictator Pol Pot designated 4/17/75 as Year Zero of his revolution, and for nearly four years he ruled the country, renamed Kampuchea, in an atmosphere of rampant terror and paranoia. An estimated two million Cambodians died from starvation and execution. Grim reminders of these atrocities can still be seen at the Tuol Sleng Prison in Phnom Penh and in the infamous Killing Fields a few miles away, now maintained as memorials by the Cambodian government.

But before the scars from this trauma have healed, another tragedy threatens to overwhelm the already weakened country: the alarming epidemic of HIV/AIDS. Two years ago there were only about six hundred reported cases of HIV in the country. Today this number has risen to an estimated one hundred and fifty thousand cases in a population of eleven million. This gives Cambodia the highest rate of HIV infection in Asia, with many studies stating that over 2.6 percent of the population are now carrying the virus. In six years, if the current trend continues, 10 percent of all Cambodians will be infected. The causes are many. Lack of education, a burgeoning sex trade industry, and a war-ravaged health care system have all made Cambodia particularly susceptible to this pandemic.

In the face of these terrible odds, Maryknoll established the Seedling of Hope project. From this small center Sister Juana Encalada, Maryknoll Father Jim Noonan, and a staff of Cambodian volunteers attempt to reach out to the local communities in a spirit of compassion.

3

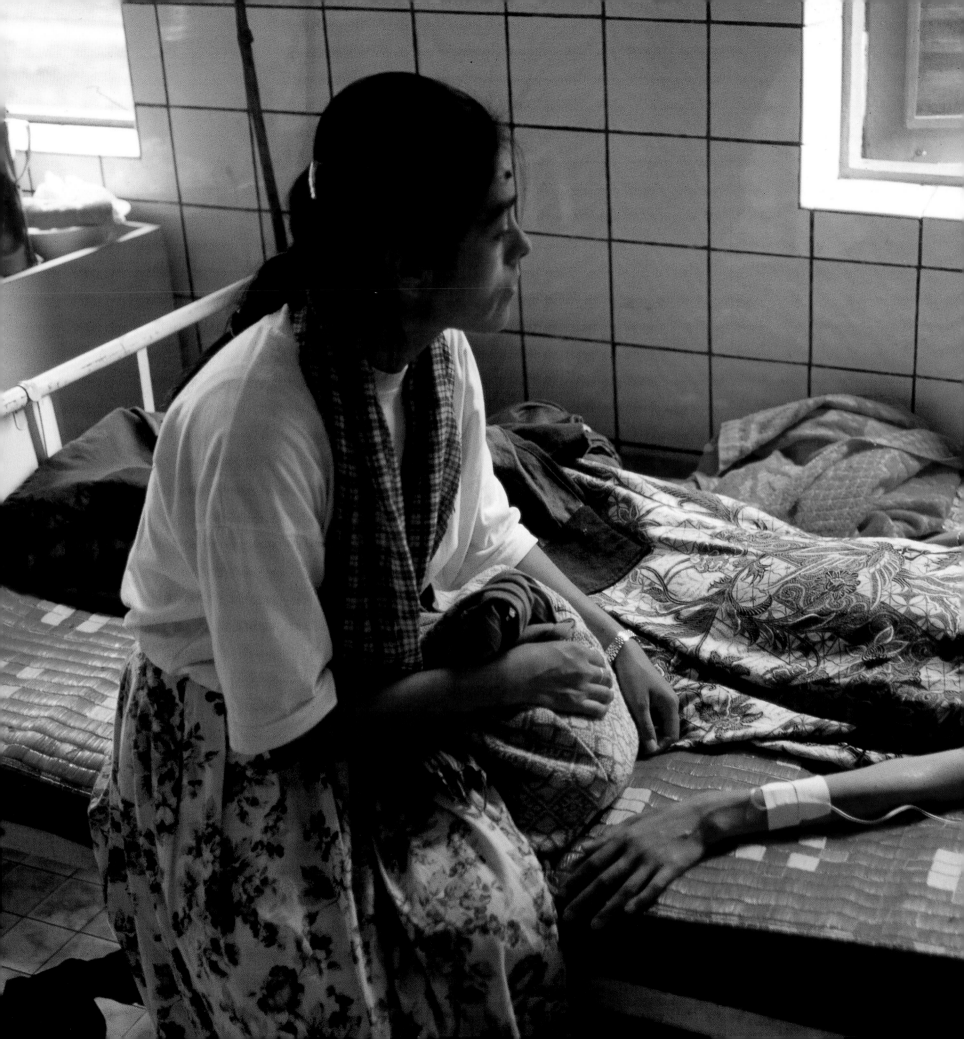

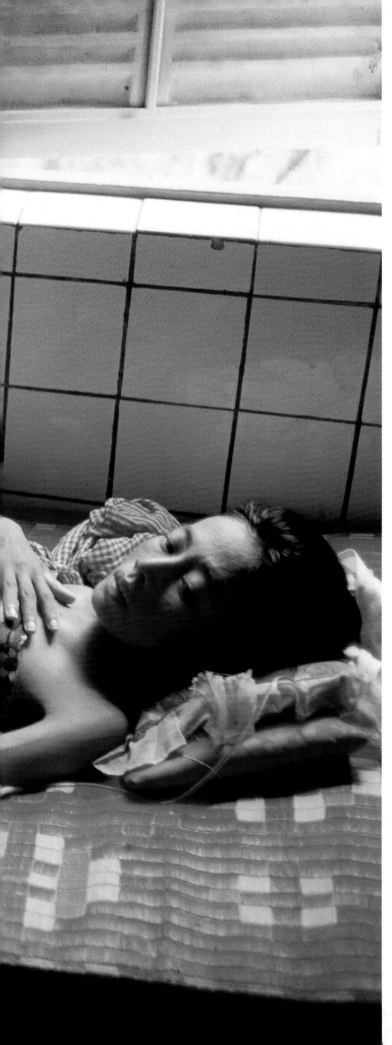

At the hospital in Phnom Penh, Encalada walks down a long, open corridor to the ward of Kun Tia, the young woman she has come to visit. From her bed Kun Tia immediately recognizes the Maryknoll Sister. Her breathing is labored and beads of sweat are breaking on her forehead. She appears much older than her twenty-nine years. Despite her weakness, she manages to bring her hands together in the familiar Cambodian greeting and flash a broad, beautiful smile. Her mother rises to greet the visitor warmly, but anxiety is written on her face.

As Encalada sits on the edge of Kun Tia's bed, the three women hold hands and begin to chat. The white curtains across the long French windows are flapping gently in the breeze. Kun Tia looks up at Juana with love in her eyes and appears to be at peace with herself as she smiles and occasionally laughs. Encalada asks a few questions about her health and listens as the dying woman expresses her concern for her young son, who sits playing on the floor a few feet away. He too has the HIV virus. The missioner assures her that he will be cared for. When it is time for her to leave Juana promises to return another day.

A few days later, she learns that Kun Tia has died. The missioner and her colleagues recall how the Cambodian woman's courage and dignity inspired them. Father Noonan describes her as "a tremendous example of someone dying with grace." A visitor asks Juana about the impact of being exposed daily to the destruction of so many lives with no power to change their fate. She realizes that she cannot alter their situation yet Encalada has learned to relate to them as valued individuals, persons whose meaning in the world goes beyond the reality of their illness and death. "I witness to the presence of God in their lives," she says.

Growing up in Arequipa, Peru, Encalada participated in the youth group in Maryknoll's Our Lady of Sorrows parish. She joined the Association of Peruvian Missionaries and worked in Tacna. There she served Aymara Indian families who migrated to the southern border town from the Peruvian highlands. Working with people of a different culture inspired the young woman to think of mission beyond her own borders. She entered the Maryknoll Sisters and, after three years of spiritual formation in the United States, she went to Cambodia in 1995. Her work with Buddhists, she says, has deepened her respect for other religions. Her work with people living with HIV/AIDS has taught her the meaning of compassion, which goes beyond religious labels. "Before you are a Christian," she says, "you must be human."

Maryknoll Sister Juana Encalada visits with Kun Tia, a Cambodian woman dying from AIDS at a hospital in Phnom Penh.

Besides currently caring for about 126 HIV/AIDS patients, Seedling of Hope conducts AIDS education programs in Phnom Penh and its surrounding villages. This has proven to be one of the center's greatest challenges. After the Khmer Rouge era, when all schools were closed and any connection with learning could lead to death, many Cambodian people remain wary of education. Their fear is exacerbated by years of isolation from the rest of the world. But slowly, Cambodians are beginning to learn about AIDS, even referring to the disease they once blamed on mosquitoes as "the world disease."

Once a week, Juana and other members of the center's staff arm themselves with pamphlets and posters explaining the risks of sexually transmitted diseases and head out to a neighborhood in the city. Today she and another young Khmer woman decide to set up their informal demonstration outside a brothel. Soon dozens of young men, many of whom are likely patrons of the establishment, gather around the two women as they begin to talk about HIV and other sexually transmitted diseases. At first the men laugh and giggle at the spectacle of the two women speaking frankly about sexual behavior while holding up posters to illustrate their presentation. But soon the laughter gives way to silence as the force of the statistics and the seriousness of the disease begin to seep in. Soon scores of men surround the women, many asking thoughtful questions.

The other Maryknoller at the center is Father Jim Noonan, 65, who grew up in Burlington, Vermont, and entered Maryknoll in 1960. Prior to his assignment to Cambodia, Noonan worked in a Maryknoll mission in the Philippines and returned to the United States to serve as Maryknoll Superior General from 1978 to 1984. He then worked in Thailand until 1991 when he transferred to Cambodia.

1

2

1 *A bottle of medicine hangs from a calendar inside the home of a woman suffering with AIDS. People with AIDS must take scores of pills a day in a battle for survival.*

2 *Juana Encalada holds up a poster illustrating the risks of AIDS as an associate talks to men outside a brothel in Phnom Penh.*

3 *Maryknollers Jim Noonan and Juana Encalada talk outside the Seedling of Hope center in downtown Phnom Penh.*

3

Noonan travels frequently from Maryknoll's Center House downtown to a small hospital in Chum Chao on the outskirts of the city. It is run by the Missionaries of Charity, the order founded by Mother Teresa of Calcutta. They also care for HIV/AIDS patients and Noonan often brings his cases here when the need arises. During the hour-long drive to the hospital with a young man with AIDS riding in the back of his car, Noonan reflects on his work and the people he assists. He says that these people often begin with a fragile self-image. Learning they have AIDS, a disease with a tremendous social stigma, makes adjustment doubly difficult. He and the other people at Seedling of Hope treat all their patients with respect, showing them that they are valuable and that they can live the rest of their lives, no matter how short, with dignity. "Working with AIDS patients is the perfect place for unconditional love," he says. "When I'm helping them to drink water or go to the bathroom, I remind myself that this is the body of Christ."

1

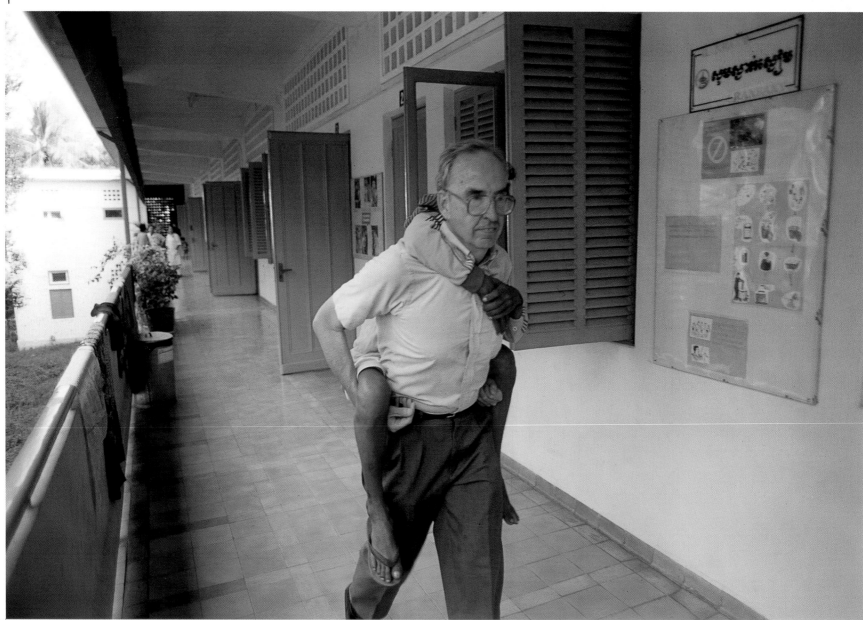

1 *Father Jim Noonan carries a sick man from his hospital room down to a waiting car where the man would be taken to another clinic to continue his care.*

2 *Encalada vists with a woman suffering from AIDS inside a modest house in Phnom Penh. Cambodia has one of the highest number of HIV/AIDS cases in the world.*

1 *Ton Thare, suffering from AIDS, sits despondently outside her home as her son peers out from the doorway.*

2 *At a small village on the outskirts of the Cambodian capital of Phnom Penh, a woman walks her bike across a bridge.*

1

IN A SMALL VILLAGE JUST SOUTH OF THE CITY, Juana Encalada is visiting another woman, Ton Thare, who is in the early stage of her illness. Unlike Kun Tia, she is visibly despondent. Two of her six children have also been diagnosed with HIV. As she crouches on the ground to talk with Juana, one son peeks out of a doorway behind her. Like 90 percent of Cambodian women who contract the disease, this woman was infected by her husband, who had probably visited a prostitute. "She's not too sick but she's depressed and sad," says Juana. "I feel sad to see her this way."

2

One night Juana Encalada reflects on her own understanding of mission, shaped by her experiences in Cambodia. She says that no matter where she serves, whether in Latin America or Asia, her first goal is to see the divine in each culture and secondly to share her life with the people she serves. The Peruvian nun says that her idea of mission has less to do with talking about her faith and more to do with simply living it. "The simple witness of other people has opened my own realization of the gift of mission, of its mystery," she says. "All of us from different cultures and religions are called to mission to each other. It's beyond religion; it's the sharing of the human spirit."

A father and son make their way across a rice paddy in a village an hour's drive outside the Cambodian capitol of Phnom Penh.

Witness
in Thailand

"How can you be with the people and not stand with them in opposition to oppressive forces that keep them disenfranchised and poor?"

— *Brother John Beeching*

John Beeching and a group of Mon monks walk along the Yadana pipeline near the Thai-Burmese border. The monks had participated in demonstrations against the construction of the controversial natural gas pipeline that involved the razing of Mon villages and serious violations of human rights.

With a visitor chasing to keep up, Brother John Beeching sprints across four lanes of Bangkok's chaotic downtown traffic to flag down a tuk-tuk, one of the city's ubiquitous motorized rickshaws. Hopping in one, he pulls his panting visitor in behind him and barks out his destination: the Buddhist temple of Wat Prok. For the next half-hour they navigate the choked streets of this perplexing city, in the process witnessing signs of the constant collision of East and West. At one point they pass a fashionably dressed businesswoman talking on a cell phone, and watch as she adroitly steps aside to avoid contact with a line of Buddhist monks filing past with their alms bowls. The next moment, a late-model Mercedes, its horn loudly blaring, waits impatiently for an old man to push his cart full of live chickens across the clogged street. Every day, through this jumble of colliding worlds, Brother John makes his way to the temple.

When Beeching first came to Bangkok in 1990 he expected to be working with AIDS patients. But this was not to be. Instead, he spends each day at Wat Prok or two other Buddhist temples in Bangkok, dividing his time between teaching English to the monks and offering medical assistance to everyone living on the temple grounds. Many of these are refugees who have escaped from ethnic oppression in neighboring Burma.

Beeching recalls that on one of his first visits to the temple he was summoned to the abbot's room. "I thought I was being called in because I had violated some point of etiquette." To his surprise, the abbot informed the Maryknoller that he wanted his monks to learn the words to the song "We Shall Overcome." It turned out that the abbot had a great regard for the American civil rights leader Martin Luther King, Jr. Beeching was surprised, knowing that Buddhist monks are not normally permitted to sing. But the abbot explained, "We shall sing this song once and then never sing again."

1

2

1 *John Beeching laughs with the abbot of Wat Prok, a Buddhist temple community in Bangkok where the Maryknoller works with Burmese refugees. The abbot, an admirer of Martin Luther King, first called on Beeching to teach his monks the words to the American spiritual "We Shall Overcome."*

2 *Beeching bargains with the driver of a tuk-tuk as he describes his destination. The three-wheeled vehicles are ubiquitous in Bangkok, used mostly by tourists, and the Maryknoll Brother uses them only as a last resort.*

3 *Inside the Wat Prok Buddhist temple community in Bangkok, young monks share a small dormitory.*

3

A group of Buddhist monks holding traditional umbrellas to shield them from the sun stroll along a beach on their way back to Bangkok after spending a few days in a refugee camp across the border in Burma.

John Beeching has been a Maryknoll Brother for over thirty years. Prior to coming to Bangkok, he spent seven years in the Middle East. This included several extremely tense years in war-ravaged Beirut, where mortar attacks and terrorist bombings were a fact of life. But it was during this time, living within an Islamic culture, that Beeching first became interested in interfaith dialogue, an interest that is avidly pursued within the old walls of Wat Prok.

John's life within a Buddhist culture has brought a profound change to his understanding of what it means to be a Maryknoll Brother. John does not hesitate to call himself a "Buddhist Christian," a reference to the synergy he senses between the two paths. Christian love and Buddhist compassion represent for him the same call to action. "Buddhists say you are a brother to that mosquito you just slapped on your wrist. The tree, the water—it's all part of what is happening to you. It's a brotherhood that embraces all of life." Increasingly it is the interior journey, rather than external geography, that characterizes his mission path. "The more I make it an interior journey the more focused I am. The Gospel says the same. But it's a concept I woke up to through Buddhism."

1

2

1 Buddhist monks ascend a long set of stairs leading to sacred caves at a shrine north of Bangkok.

2 A three-year-old Mon girl dances along as a troupe of dancers perform at a refugee camp on the Thai-Burmese border.

3 Two monks pray at a Buddhist shrine located inside a cave in Thailand north of Bangkok. In the safety of the cave, one monk wore the red robes of his native Burma, something he would not normally do as it identifies him as an "illegal" refugee.

3

1   *A Mon doctor treats an elderly woman at the health care clinic at the Holockhani refugee camp in Burma. Members of Doctors Without Borders have a presence at the camp and help staff and supply the clinic.*

2   *A young Mon girl performs as part of a troupe of dancers who are entertaining fellow Burmese refugees at a camp near the Thai-Burmese border.*

3   *During the sweltering heat of mid-day in Bangkok, a Buddhist monk cools himself by a window at the Wat Prok temple. John Beeching, who had spent the morning at the temple, puts his shoes back on as he prepares to leave.*

He adds that to work with people with the single motivation of converting them is cynical "conditional love" that is ultimately un-Christian. He says that for him living his own faith requires total respect for another's faith and spirituality. At the same time, Beeching says that the work of missioners is typically with the marginalized people of the world, and this demands action. "How can you be with the people and not stand with them in opposition to the oppressive forces that keep them disenfranchised and poor?"

Much of Brother John's work at the temple involves accompanying the Mon refugees who have sought protection at Wat Prok. The Mon are an indigenous Burmese people who are being brutalized by the ruling military regime of Burma (or Myanmar, the country's current official name). Beeching has chosen to walk with the Mon, as well as other Burmese ethnic groups, as an expression of his role as a Brother. He joins them on marches and demonstrations in front of the Myanmar embassy in Bangkok, helps in securing visas and passports, and assists them in getting supplies to some of the refugee camps along the Burmese-Thai border. It is a basic respect for human rights, enhanced by his embrace of Buddhist and Christian principles, that fuels Beeching's considerable passion and at times puts the Maryknoller in direct conflict with the authorities.

He recalls the time, one of many, that the Thai police raided Wat Prok in an effort to gather up illegal aliens, mainly Mon people, for whom forced repatriation would entail great danger. One of the refugees picked up that day was not only blind but also missing both hands. Incensed by the absurdity of the situation, Beeching stormed over to the police station and loudly confronted the arresting officer. Surprised by Beeching's audacity, the officer justified the arrest by stating that the man might take a job away from a Thai citizen. At that, the Maryknoller yelled, "This man has no hands and is blind. What type of a job do you think he'd take? A policeman's job?" He then abruptly left the police station, lucky not to have been arrested on the spot.

3

A mother and her children wait for treatment at the health care clinic inside the Holockhani camp.

1

2

ON A LONG, DUSTY ROAD that winds through the mountains of northeastern Thailand, Beeching and a group of refugees approach the last of five Thai army checkpoints as they make their way to the Mon's Holockhani refugee camp, just across the Burmese boarder. As the old Toyota pickup comes to a halt, a young Thai soldier, his machine gun held at the ready, grimly inspects the passengers who respond by clasping their hands together and bowing their heads in greeting. Inside the truck, apart from the driver, are Beeching and a Western visitor, seven Mon people, as well as piles of food and supplies. The soldier immediately questions the driver, especially about the two Westerners. Some anxious minutes pass, along with the transfer of some cigarettes and other gifts, until the soldier abruptly waves the truck on. A mile later, the group crests a hill and descends into the camp, marked by a tattered Burmese flag stuck in the ground.

Among those accompanying Beeching is Pra Tissa, a Buddhist monk and Mon refugee, who eagerly returns to the camp in spite of the very real risk of repatriation. Together they tour the camp, walking along the dirt road that passes hundreds of ramshackle bamboo houses and an occasional well where children play in the water. Men huddling in the shadows of their homes extend greetings to the visitors. When two old people drop to their knees in the dirt and ask for the young monk's blessing he cheerfully lays a hand on each head.

The visitors make their way to the camp's hospital where two French doctors, members of the humanitarian group Doctors Without Borders, are tending to patients. Mothers wait their turn with their children, their faces sprinkled with the gold powder that is a common Burmese beauty aid. The scene is remarkable for its peacefulness despite the fact that only five kilometers away is the base of the Burmese Army's Light Infantry Battalion, the same soldiers who recently set fire to the camp and who regularly abduct "recruits" for army duty or for slave labor on various government projects.

One of those projects is the infamous Yadana pipeline, built by the government of Myanmar to sell natural gas to Thailand. After their visit to the camp Beeching, Tissa, and two other Mon monks stop by the pipeline to walk along the huge conduit that snakes over the ground. The pipeline's construction has brought great misery to the indigenous Burmese villagers along its path, and many groups, including the Mon, are fighting its existence. In some cases, whole villages were relocated or razed to make way for the project and thousands of people were pressed into slave labor. The construction companies, one French and the other American, have been accused of profiting from this deplorable situation, even as they deny any connection to abuses. The orange-robed monks and their North American companion make for a highly conspicuous group, and within a few minutes they are confronted by an official from Total, the French company working on the construction, who forces them off the property. They hop back in their van and head back quickly to Bangkok, fearful that some zealous Thai official might detain them and decide to return the monks to Burma.

Seven hours later the monks are back at Wat Prok, and Beeching reflects on his unique mission. Sitting inside the dark wood paneled rooms of the old temple, he recalls a difficult time when a young man died in his arms. Several years ago the monks brought Ngai, a twenty-four-year-old Mon who was suffering from malaria, to see Beeching. "He was just skin and bones. I realized he was dying and I kept him breathing with mouth-to-mouth." John took the man to the hospital and had him admitted. After three days the hospital informed him that they could save Ngai but it would cost $40,000. Beeching said that all of his money had already been used up and begged them to reconsider. The hospital refused, and so Ngai was taken off his respirator and Beeching returned with him to Wat Prok.

"I asked Ngai if he understood I was taking him back to the temple and that he was dying. He grabbed my wrist. I told him he is a good man and that he had gained a lot of merit. I said that everything would be Okay and that he could let go. Twenty minutes later he died." As he tells the story, tears well up in John's eyes.

Looking back on it, Beeching knows there was a lot of anguish and pain in being so helpless to save this man, but at the same time he realized that he was witnessing the Gospel. He said that at that moment he realized that there wasn't a separate Christian world or a Buddhist world; there was only one brotherhood. "That was the body of Christ I was holding in my arms."

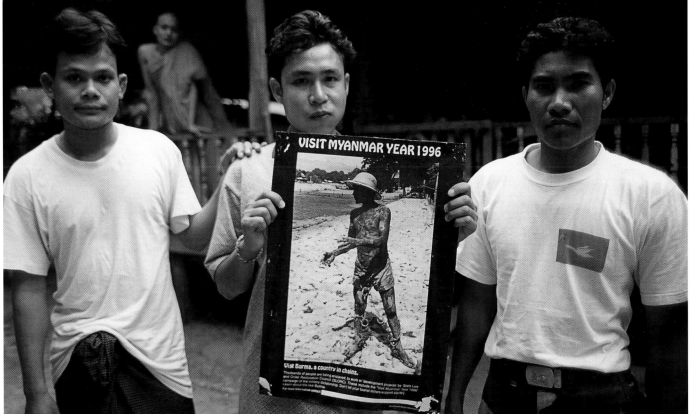

1 John Beeching stops to talk with young members of a Karen refugee camp on the Thai-Burmese border. As with the nearby Mon camp, these refugees are subject to periodic harassment from both Burmese and Thai troops.

2 Workers apply new sections of straw thatch to a roof of a home in a village that sits on the Burmese-Thai border. This area of Thailand, referred to as the Borderland, is made up mostly of ethnic Burmese refugees who have escaped war and oppression in their native land.

3 Inside the Holockhani camp, a refugee leans out of his window. The camp is settled by people who were forced from their villages by war and military intimidation.

4 Volunteers at the Mon Refugee Center in Sangklaburi, Thailand, a few miles from Burma, hold up a poster mocking the Burmese military's attempt to lure tourists to Burma (Myanmar). The poster shows a man in chains in one of the many forced-labor camps in Burma.

Signs on the Serengeti

"With the harshness and poverty around us, prayer becomes my anchor here. God helps me be a good neighbor."

— *Peter Kailing*

Johanna Kailing uses her experience as a special needs educator to work with Jose Ndarro at his home in Mugumu, Tanzania. As Jose's younger brother watches, she uses challenging games to help Jose with his coordination and language skills.

As Maryknoll lay missioners Peter and Johanna Kailing approach the mud brick house, eleven-year-old Jose Ndarro rushes out to meet the couple, grabs Johanna's hand, and excitedly signs a greeting to her. Johanna beams as the deaf boy leads her back to where his parents and siblings await them outside their home. Wooden chairs are brought out for the visitors and placed in a circle in the dirt. "Karibu!" Jose's mother Letecia calls out, welcoming the guests in Kiswahili as the adults settle into the ritual of exchanging greetings. Jose sits smiling on his stool, his arms floating about in unruly spasms, and fixes his eyes on Johanna.

As part of her mission to Mugumu, this remote Tanzanian village on the edge of the famed Serengeti Game Park, Johanna has been helping the young boy deal with his silent world by developing his motor skills and teaching him sign language. In impoverished Tanzania, where basic education is often a luxury, physically challenged children like Jose are largely ignored. In response, the young Maryknoller has used her training in special education to help address the distinct needs of these children.

Using funds from Maryknoll as well as from private and public organizations, Johanna Kailing helped start one of the first special education classrooms in Tanzania within the school district of Serengeti. "Families have no classroom for their disabled children. We've visited fifty families in this area and they are very happy because an education that was unavailable before is now available in their district." As a creative solution, Johanna approached the Serengeti Regional Conservation Strategy, an organization committed to preserving the Serengeti Park, to donate money to Mugumu as part of that organization's effort to assist villages that border the park. Additionally, an advertisement that ran in *Maryknoll* magazine raised $2,000 for the project.

Johanna turns her attention to the boy who has been squirming on his seat, and the two begin to sign to each other. Jose, giggling and laughing, gets up to lead Johanna, Pete and a visitor into his house. It's a typically modest Mugumu home built of mud bricks and tin. Inside the dark house, lit from a single small window on one wall, Johanna pulls out flash cards from her bag and holds them up to Jose, who struggles to sign the words while fighting to control his twisting body. Family members crowd into the little room to watch and Jose, clearly pleased with all the attention he is getting, sits back and giggles. Johanna patiently waits for Jose's twitching to subside before calling his attention to the next card. "He's a happy kid," Johanna says afterward. "It's nice to see him. It's been two months since I was here and I see a lot of improvement. I knew before we came to Mugumu that this was a place that didn't get a lot done when it came to the disabled."

1

1 While the classrooms at the school in Mugumu, Tanzania are modest with a tin roof and a dirt floor, the teachers and students take education seriously.

2 A boy runs to catch up with his classmates at a school in Mugumu. Being late for school has painful consequences for pupils as the penalty is a very hard slap on the hand with a long stick.

3 A student listens intently as a teacher calls on him to answer a question during class at the school in Mugumu.

Johanna has also taken up the issue of corporal punishment in Tanzanian schools. It is completely accepted practice to cane a child for tardiness or other infractions. It is common to see groups of children in their uniforms kneeling in the dirt of the schoolyard as a teacher brandishing a switch gives each a solid smack across the hand. Johanna says, "Forty kids show up late for school one morning and the teacher makes them all kneel down and whack, whack, whack, they all get the cane." In January of 1998, she helped organize a conference of teachers that searched for nonviolent disciplinary alternatives.

3

2

1

1 Peter Kailing and Charles Sampson became close friends during the three years that the Kailings lived in Mugumu. While walking down a street in town, Charles (left) shares a joke with Peter.

2 Peter and Johanna sit to talk with the Ndarro family outside their home in Mugumu. Their son Jose, who is deaf and has learning difficulties, has special education needs that Johanna helps address during her weekly visits.

3 Peter and Charles inspect one of their corn plants in a field outside Mugumu. The field is part of an experimental project intended to introduce modern agricultural practices to the community.

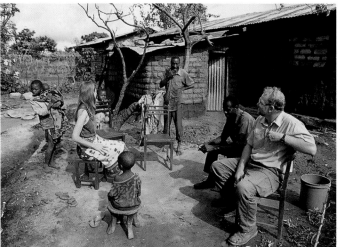

2

Johanna and her husband Peter Kailing first met at a religious retreat in Milwaukee in 1991. They were married two years later and came to Tanzania together as Maryknoll lay missioners in 1995. Johanna had been with Maryknoll for thirteen years, serving ten years in Taiwan and another three years in development in Chicago. But for Peter this was his first Maryknoll assignment.

Peter grew up on a dairy farm in Michigan and, after graduating from Michigan State, worked with the rural poor in Appalachia. It was there that he discovered his desire to help the underprivileged. "I wanted to be of service, to help make the world a better place." He also realized that he wanted to work in a religious group. "I wanted to be identified as a Christian. I believe in the Gospel. It's not like I'm whacking anybody over the head with the Bible. But I'm a Christian. So here I am."

Working alongside Tanzanians who share his interest in agriculture, Peter helps administer a seventy-acre farm outside of Mugumu that is rented by the Diocese of Musoma. The raising of crops on the farm helps to teach new growing techniques while providing food for Mugumu's technical school, "Chipuka," which means "to grow." However, running a farm in Tanzania entails challenges he never faced in Michigan.

While walking through the fields, Peter and Charlie Sampson, his Tanzanian assistant, turn toward the farm house, wading cautiously through tall grass, keeping a sharp eye out for black mambas, deadly snakes that can move almost as fast as a man can run. They stop to look at the plow and are dismayed to find that the tiny brass fittings of the lubrication ports, hidden in the grass underneath the plow (and worth only a few cents), have been stolen. So desperate are the needs of the Tanzanians that thievery is a constant and challenging problem. The lug nuts on the diocese's Toyota truck are locked onto the wheel and the spare tire sports a heavy, thick chain. Routine trips into town for supplies are always done with great vigilance so that purchases are not openly displayed and everything is completely lashed down in the bed of the truck.

3

Some of these conditions, while daunting enough by themselves, have also raised moral questions for the Kailings. Their mission is to live a Christian life among their neighbors, helping as much as they can while being careful not to create an attitude of dependency. It's a delicate balance for the Maryknoll missioners. Often they are administering large sums of money targeted for projects such as building a special education classroom or the planting of trees. In Tanzania, where per capita income is pitifully small, the Kailings are sensitive not to be perceived as a funnel for cash. Their aim is rather to foster self-reliance. Johanna explains, "As a missioner, I've been very challenged by the harshness of living here, the poverty around us. There are many ways to give, but what's the right way? How do I participate in something that works toward solving problems with Tanzanians?" For the Kailings, the answers usually demand a certain sensitivity and adjustment to the facts of life in Tanzania. Their life here has been a series of such adjustments.

A group of young Masai tribesmen on their way to a celebration walk toward their village near the Ngorongoro Crater in Tanzania.

ONE OF THE FACTS OF LIFE IN TANZANIA is constant crowding. People rarely do anything by themselves, and their reliance on each other is both a survival mechanism and a tribal tradition. In fact, so strong is the custom of being in the company of others that the need for occasional solitude or privacy is looked upon with suspicion and deep mistrust. For the Kailings, coming from America, this was an aspect of the culture that took time to appreciate.

With scores of daily visitors to the Kailing home, the couple often find themselves longing for some time alone. Peter recalls how, after one particularly crowded day at home, he decided to go for a walk outside of town. With a master's degree in wildlife biology, he deeply loves the outdoors and looks for any opportunity to view the many exotic animals that live within the Serengeti district. On this occasion he simply walked a short distance from his house and found a quiet place on the side of a grassy bank commanding a beautiful view of the rolling green hills bordering the Serengeti Park. After only a few moments of quiet reflection in the warm sunshine, a few neighbors suddenly appeared and sat with him. "What are you doing?" one of them asked. Peter replied simply, "I just wanted to be alone." By this point a few more neighbors had appeared and gathered around. "What's wrong? Are you sick?" they inquired with concern. His solitude broken, Peter decided just to relax and take in the scene with his friends.

Johanna recalls the time when they decided to celebrate their wedding anniversary by spending the night camping on an isolated hill, not far from the farm. They picked the location for the exact reason that it was out of town and would give them a much needed retreat. After hiking for part of the day, they pitched their tent on top of a steep hill, ate dinner, and eventually turned in for the night. The next morning they walked back down to the farm only to be met by a gathering of concerned villagers who had spent the night looking for them. "Where have you been?" they asked. "We were all worried when we couldn't find you." After reassuring them that they had simply spent the night in a tent, one man asked, with evident dismay, "Why would you do that when you have a house?" "And why," asked another man incredulously, "would you want to be out there alone?"

1

2

1 *After the rains of spring fall on Tanzania, the once dry countryside explodes from brown to green almost overnight. Here, a boy walks along a road near Arusha, Tanzania.*

2 *Two young Masai girls share a laugh outside their home near Ngorongoro, Tanzania.*

3 *A typical farm house seen along the road to Arusha, Tanzania.*

3

1 *A sudden rainstorm doesn't seem to dampen the spirits of a Masai tribesman as he runs home along the hills near the Serengeti.*

2 *Young Masai girls provide harmony while a group of young men dance and sing during a celebration in a village in Tanzania.*

1

THE KAILINGS FEEL EXTREMELY PRIVILEGED to be so close to the famed Serengeti Park, a game preserve roughly the size of Connecticut. Frequently they drive their truck along the dirt road "game drives" to observe and photograph the herds of wildebeests and zebra, the families of lions, or the majestic elephants that march freely across the plains. It is also an opportunity to visit different tribes, such as the cattle-herding Masai, whose red robes contrast so dramatically with the stunningly green grass. During one visit, Peter and Johanna visited a Masai village and watched a celebration where young men dressed in silver necklaces and carrying long spears formed a circle, jumping and singing a haunting dirge.

Having their own vehicle and being residents of Tanzania enable them to navigate the park at their own leisure, while avoiding the high cost of joining a private tour and the expensive non-resident park fees. At the same time, as they are on their own, the couple takes the time to educate themselves about the wonders and dangers of visiting a park full of free-roaming predators.

While touring the park with a guest from Maine, the three of them make their first stop a riverbed where scores of hippos cool themselves by lolling in the muddy water. Once out of the truck Peter and Johanna begin taking photographs of the enormous animals from the top of the bank while their American friend walks to the water's edge for a closer look. In a calm voice, Peter calls out, "Uh, you might not want to stand there, Jim. Crocodiles watch the shore by lying just under the water and they burst through the surface in a split second." Without hesitating their friend bolts for the top of the bank, his face flushed and his heart beating fast, while Peter continues his matter-of-fact warning. "They grab you and pull you out into the middle of the river where they take you to the bottom and then wait for you to drown. Then they eat you." For the rest of the visit, their friend stays close to his Maryknoll guides.

2

During their three years in Mugumu, both Peter and Johanna established strong relationships with their neighbors, close friendships that made their planned departure from the village all the more difficult. Like all members of the Maryknoll Mission Association of the Faithful, the Kailings had signed a three-year contract, and theirs was due to expire in the spring of 1998. Although they could renew for another three years, they chose to return to the States where family concerns called them home. Saying goodbye to the village was a difficult experience.

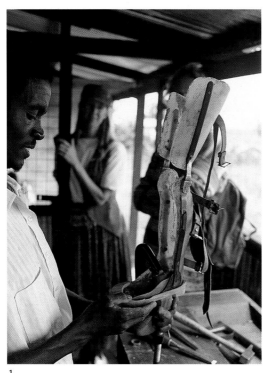
1

Johanna had worked closely with Nemes Sianga, the principal of the school in Mugumu. When it came time to tell him about their plans to leave, Johanna spoke to him in the schoolyard one morning while children arrived for the start of the school day. As Johanna carefully explained her reasons for leaving, the principal was visibly affected, listening with his head bowed while staring at the ground. When she finished, they briefly embraced. He responded as did many others who heard the news of their leaving, with kindness and a little bewilderment.

Once news of their upcoming departure spread through the village, people gathered outside the Kailings' home. Although their departure was a couple of months away, they wanted to give themselves as well their friends and neighbors time to adjust to their leaving. Some came asking for items they might leave behind; others simply asking for a postcard or a picture of their family when they got back to the United States. One terribly crippled man, who moved along practically on all fours, made his way from a long distance just to speak one more time with Johanna and Peter.

Gestures like this reminded the Kailings of the importance Africans place on relationship, and they were glad to know that their presence had made a difference in the lives of their neighbors. Peter recalled one night when he was awakened by his friend Simon, who was whispering his name outside the window. It turned out that Simon's wife, Martha, was delivering a baby and needed help. Peter quickly dressed and drove where Simon directed him to a field on the outskirts of town. "All I could gather from Simon's words was some problem with the umbilical cord. When we got there I saw the spot where she had given birth. It was on the edge of a field just off the dirt road. In the bright moonlight I could easily see the soaked patched of earth, darker than the dark ground." Rather than rush to the hospital, Simon simply asked Pete to drive him and Martha back home.

Later that night Peter returned to their house and learned that both the mother and baby were fine. The child, a girl, had been given a tribal name that means "one who was born in a field." All this prompted Peter to write in his journal, "Tonight has been one of those uncommon experiences that you need once in a while when you know in your gut and soul that you belong, that you have done well, and that being a missioner has its occasional transcendent moments."

1 Johanna Kailing visits a Mugumu shop that makes artificial limbs for physically disabled Tanzanians. The shop is supported by a group from the Netherlands which runs a community-based rehabilitation program that Johanna assists.

2 A Muslim man looks over an impressive collection of dress shoes at an outdoor market off the dirt streets of Mugumu. The small town, just outside the Serengeti National Park, is a six-hour, rattling drive from the nearest city.

Back in Big Rapids, Michigan, where Johanna and Peter are now raising their baby daughter, both reflect on how their experiences in mission in Tanzania are translating into their new lives in America. Johanna reflects on her involvement with her local church, where she's training to assist people at times of crisis. "Getting involved with my parish at home would be my primary way to be connected to mission. It's being a Christian neighbor and a trustworthy listener."

Peter says, "I miss the easy exchange and relaxed engagement of speaking with Tanzanians. I try to incorporate that gift of intensive listening and patience with folks I encounter here. I have regained a profound sense of gratefulness… appreciating what has become commonplace in America—clean water to drink, food year around, dependable jobs. We have so much to thank God for."

1

1 *A woman walks past a building after shopping at the outdoor vegetable market in Mugumu.*

2 *A group of young Masai men pause briefly from singing and dancing during a celebration at their village near Ngorongoro, Tanzania.*

Closing
the Divide

"Faith is a search, an open attitude that brings moments of discovery. We search together with the people for the presence of God."

— *Sister Melinda Roper*

Beverly Arao (left) and Melinda Roper talk about their plans for a tilapia fish farm at their ranch in Santa Fe, Panama. Tilapia are a fast-growing fish that can be grown in shallow pools. They are an attractive source of protein for rural communities around the world.

Driving fast along the road to Darien from Panama City, Maryknoll Sister Beverly Arao lets out a whoop as her Toyota pickup leaps onto the dirt where the paved section of the highway ends. She barely changes speed. With the choking chaos of the city behind her, the lush green mountains of Panama's most rural province rise abruptly into the sky. Men on sturdy horses trot along the rugged road, some nodding their heads in greeting as the truck roars by. As she approaches the town of Agua Fría #1, two *vaqueros* (cowboys) are driving a large herd of white cattle off the side of the road, their saddles and wide hats covered in a mantle of dust. If it weren't for the soldiers with submachine guns standing at a roadblock, you'd think you were in Texas.

Beverly stops her truck and a young soldier wearing olive green fatigues and a stern expression slowly approaches the car. He has the swagger one often sees in the military of the third world, especially in Latin America. He recognizes the Maryknoll nun, whose monthly trips to the city from Darien have made her a common sight along the road, and he turns his attention to the blond, blue-eyed visitor traveling with her.

While examining his passport and tourist card the soldier asks questions about date of arrival, purpose of visit, and length of stay. He returns the papers and waves the nun on. After pulling away, the visitor asks Arao why the soldier singled him out. "You're a gringo!" Beverly yells with a hearty laugh. The American nun, born and raised in Los Angeles by Japanese parents, enjoys the irony that her oriental features and Spanish fluency lead many Panamanians to assume she's a native.

1

2

1 With the sun setting, two men stand near their home in a remote part of Darien, the most rural province in Panama.

2 Beverly Arao often uses a horse to reach remote villages with no roads. A young girl jumped on this horse as the Maryknoll nun rode to the village to baptize two children into the Catholic faith.

3 Life is hard for the indigenous people of Panama who must fight poverty and prejudice at the same time. Despite the hardships, evidence of close family ties is everywhere.

3

MARYKNOLL SISTERS BEVERLY ARAO AND MELINDA ROPER (along with Maryknoll Sister Jocelyn Fenix) live on a communal farm in Santa Fe, a small village in the province of Darien. They work with the local community, which consists mainly of farmers and people from indigenous tribes. The nuns address the needs of the people at many levels by offering workshops on such topics as sustainable agriculture, spirituality, and women's rights. These are elements of a pastoral strategy designed to promote community well-being and cooperation. According to Melinda Roper, it is a way for the Maryknoll nuns "to live our faith in an integral way."

The centerpiece of their effort is an innovative organization known by its Spanish acronym, ECODIC, which is a Christian community dedicated to personal and communal development. The organization promotes organic farming techniques that nourish rather than deplete the land and has set up ways to market produce directly to consumers, thereby avoiding middlemen, and raising profits for the farming community. Members of the farm have also recently started raising tilapia, a nutritious freshwater fish that has become an increasingly popular source of protein in developing countries. They have built an ingenious system of holding ponds and dikes that enables the fast-growing fish to thrive inside rice paddies. The fish will provide not only food but also a viable cash crop for the organization. At the same time this project teaches members about irrigation and how to grow and harvest rice in water rather than by the traditional dry method used by most Panamanians.

ECODIC came about as a result of a survey of needs conducted by the Maryknollers with members of the twenty-three communities in their district. They learned that the people lacked sufficient nutrition and effective, renewable farming practices. The nuns also learned that, due to the circumstances that brought most of the people to Darien, the majority desired a greater sense of community. Until recently this area was inhabited primarily by indigenous Indians. The non-indigenous Panamanians first came to Darien only within the last twenty years, searching for arable land and greater opportunity. However, this same pioneer spirit that gave them the courage to uproot and relocate to a strange place has also bred a strong individualism and contributed to their isolation from one another. The ECODIC program relies on team-building principles in all of its efforts as a way to curb isolation and encourage community.

1

1 *Maryknoll Sister Melinda Roper talks to a group of catechists in the town of Tamarindo in Darien, Panama.*

2 *Melinda Roper, former president of the Maryknoll Sisters, carries a chicken that is about to become dinner at the ranch in Santa Fe, Panama.*

3 *Members of ECODIC, a Christian development community, work together to weed a cooperative field on land at the ranch where Maryknoll Sisters Arao and Roper live. Work and proceeds from crop sales are shared among members.*

4 *Beverly Arao, a Japanese-American, studies Eastern philosophy and practices Chinese movement techniques. Here she leads Melinda and guests in meditation and movement at their ranch in Santa Fe.*

The indigenous people of Darien had to adjust to the sudden influx of pioneers along with the inevitable stress that accompanies development. Traditional slash and burn agriculture along with the use of chemicals was destroying the land and rivers and compromising the natural habitat of the tribe's food source. The Maryknoll Sisters sought to address these concerns through workshops on sustainable agriculture, conflict resolution, interpersonal relationships, family dynamics, and women's rights.

The ECODIC farm consists of a group of buildings, all arranged in a campus style, including a dining hall, library, and two large dorms with long lines of bunk beds for the many guests who come to participate in workshops, or to be trained as catechists or as lay ministers. Others come simply to observe and learn about this unique community. A large, open-air hall crowns the top of a round building in the center of the farm, its design inspired by the open homes of Panamanian tribes. The space is used for group discussions, workshops, and meditation. Beverly, who draws on her knowledge of Eastern philosophy and traditions, also uses the space to lead small gatherings in Qi Gong, an ancient Chinese practice of movement and meditation.

4

2

3

A man shows off two pet parrots he keeps in his home in a rural village inside a rain forest in Darien, Panama.

A young girl tends the cooking fire inside the round, open-walled home of her Emberá family in Panama.

Sister Beverly Arao grew up in Southern California in a Japanese-American family. While her mother was Buddhist and her father was Baptist, neither was religiously active. She says that the first time she heard about Christ was from a six-year-old neighbor who decided that Beverly, who was seven at the time, should be baptized. "She baptized me with a garden hose in the back yard," the Maryknoll nun recalls with much laughter. Ten years later Arao was officially baptized in a Catholic church and eventually she entered the Maryknoll Sisters in 1987. In the presence of family and friends who traveled to Panama for the occasion, Arao made her final vows in the little church in Santa Fe in 1997.

Melinda Roper grew up in Chicago and entered Maryknoll in 1957, making her own final vows in Mexico, where she was working in the city of Mérida in the Yucatan. She worked in Mexico and Guatemala for fifteen years and was elected president of the Maryknoll Sisters in 1978, an office she held until 1984. It was during her term that the Maryknoll Sisters experienced one of their terrible crises: the brutal murder of Sisters Maura Clarke and Ita Ford by a military death squad in El Salvador. It was a time of tremendous loss and suffering for Maryknoll, and many recall with admiration the faith and courage reflected in Roper's call for "forgiving hearts." Referring to her fallen sisters, she observed, "The wisdom of their faith was that their lives were not focused against evil but upon the holiness of human life." This was a philosophy she took with her when she was assigned to Panama in 1985.

Both Maryknoll Sisters say that their journeys as missioners began "with a fascination of who God could be" and that their motivation as nuns has as much to do with a personal search for mystery as it does with mission. "We discover the beauty and tragedy of life together," Roper says.

In 1998, Roper herself experienced the power of God when a routine trip to a mission meeting turned into a harrowing and tragic event. Melinda, along with the bishop, a group of nine religious workers, and two local policemen, journeyed to Jaque on the Pacific coast near the Colombian border. At the town of La Palma, the group climbed into a large dugout canoe in the pre-dawn dark and pushed off into a surging sea for an eight-hour ride down the coast. Sister Mercedes Perez, a Dominican nun from Colombia, was particularly nervous about the journey. By ten o'clock the canoe approached Jaque, where the beach was being pounded by enormous, twelve-meter-high surf.

"It was very difficult," Roper recalls. "We were waiting in the water for a lull when the next wave turned us sideways and the boat sank. We were a half a kilometer from the shore." Clinging to a life preserver, the exhausted Maryknoll nun finally let herself be carried to shore where waiting hands lifted her to safety. "Moments before we went down, I turned and saw Mercedes sitting behind me and I noticed how nervous she was. They found her body a few days later."

The impact of the accident settled on Roper for the first time when she and other missioners traveled to Mercedes's village the next week. "There was a celebration for her and it was full of life," she recalls. On such occasions, "One realizes the whole miracle and precariousness of life."

The Sisters go on to discuss how the political situation in Panama influences their philosophies of mission. They say that in Latin America there has been a re-reading of the Gospel, in which the story of Jesus, especially his advocacy for the poor and his struggles with the power structures of his day, has taken on greater meaning. As with many countries in Latin America, Panama has long been run by the rich and powerful with little regard for the suffering of the poor. The call of the church in Latin America to stand up for the poor is a call these two women have felt compelled to accept personally.

For nearly a hundred years Panama has been distinguished by the Canal Zone, a ten-mile-long swath of territory that until recently has literally cut the country in two. Administered until January 1, 2000 by the United States, the Canal had come to symbolize the division within the collective psyche of Panamanians. According to the Sisters, Panamanians have lived so long under the influence of the United States that they question their own identity. Now that the Canal has reverted back to Panama's control it is hoped that the country will come together again. Divisions still linger, however, over the U.S. invasion in 1989. While many Panamanians were just as glad to be rid of strongman Manuel Noriega, the invasion also exacerbated national feelings of helplessness and a sense of the country's inability to take care of itself.

Beverly Arao remembers the day clearly. On December 19, 1989, she had only been in Panama City for three days, having arrived from Guatemala to begin her new Maryknoll assignment. She was with a group of Maryknoll nuns inside their house in Las Mañanitas, a small village just outside Panama City. They had just finished a Christmas party around eleven o'clock at night when they began hearing planes overhead. "We walked outside and in the sky was a long line of planes flying above us with no lights," Arao recalls. At about 12:45 the bombs started to fall and machine gun fire erupted throughout the city.

By the next morning, moments after President Bush's announcement of the invasion of Panama was broadcast on the armed forces television station, families began leaving the city in droves and looters began attacking downtown stores. The Maryknoll nuns remained indoors for the next couple of days until a Salvadoran friend came to the house and told the nuns they had to leave. "You've got to get out of here," he said. "Noriega's people are looking for Americans." The Sisters got a ride to a U.S. post near the airport where they were put up in a hangar converted into temporary living quarters. Beverly, a trained nurse, made her way to the hospital in the city to volunteer her services.

1

At the hospital Arao witnessed first-hand the confusion of an undeclared war. Elderly patients who had jumped through windows to escape the fires raging in their homes were being treated for burns and injuries while a U.S. soldier walked calmly among other terrified patients stopping to write "E" on a few foreheads with a red felt pen. Arao later learned that the E stood for "enemy." "There was this one nurse who got really angry at the soldier," she recalls. "She screamed at him that the people were frightened and what he was doing was terrible. I was impressed by her."

After the invasion, which devastated the city and claimed many more lives than the official U.S. statistics stated, Beverly felt a great deal of empathy for the people of Panama. When she was working in Guatemala massacres had been a weekly occurrence and now the events in Panama drew her closer to the people. "I felt like I wanted to identify with the Panamanians. We did a lot of pastoral reflection (with the community) on the invasion. We talked about U.S. policy and the injustice of the invasion." Arao said that the invasion helped galvanize her commitment to the people. The appreciation and love of the people she serves is in evidence when the Maryknoll Sister visits one of the communities in their area.

3

1 Outside a hardware store in Santa Fe, a woman nurses her child.

2 As is often the case in poor communities in Latin America, horses are valuable commodities.

3 While visiting a tribal village, a young friend runs over to Beverly to give her a hug as she is about to leave the village.

2

1

1 *A mother and her two daughters wait for her husband to return from the sugar cane fields in their village in Darien, Panama.*

2 *Beverly Arao visits an Emberá family in their village near Agua Fria. The Maryknoll nun makes a point of visiting communities on a regular basis.*

3 *Under the protection of their raised house, a man and his small son share a hammock.*

SAN MIGUEL IS A SMALL COMMUNITY OF CATTLE FARMERS located about ten kilometers from the road in Santa Fe and accessible only by a trail that winds through jungle and groves of teak. Beverly Arao, accompanied by Maryknoll Affiliate Patti Morrison, has come to the village to perform two baptisms and as she emerges out of the jungle and into the clearing of San Miguel, small children run up to greet her. Neighbors call out to her from their modest, dirt-floor homes as she passes. With two small girls leading the way, Beverly arrives at the home of Ramiro Trejos. Within minutes a meal of rice and chicken is offered, which Arao gratefully accepts. As she eats, the house slowly fills with the people of the town, most of whom are related: cousins, aunts, uncles and grandparents. The arrangements for the next day's baptismal celebration are the principal topic of discussion.

Late in the day, with a moonless night overhead, Beverly, Ramiro, and his wife and two daughters spend the last few hours before bedtime sitting around the candle-light, playing word games and sharing easy conversation. Morrison teaches the girls "Simon Dice" (Simon Says) and the girls teach her a favorite rhyme, much to the delight of the squealing girls and the laughing parents who look on from their hammocks. It's a gentle scene of a family relaxing at the end of the day, and an American nun, who is so lovingly and naturally embraced within the circle.

3

2

Attending a
Wounded Land

"There's a tremendous need for doctors here.
I feel this is where I need to be."

— Susan Nagele

*Dr. Susan Nagele listens as a Toposa woman explains some of
the medical problems that members of her tribe are having at a
village near Narus, southern Sudan.*

EBONY-COLORED WOMEN DRESSED IN ANIMAL HIDES fringed with colorful beads sit on the ground, rigorously shaking gourds of milk suspended from cords of cow intestines. Behind them the sun drops behind the Didinga Hills near Narus in southern Sudan, casting a warm glow over thatched huts whose domed roofs and spindly legs make them look like giant beehives on stilts. A handful of naked children, chasing chickens across the yard, pause in their play and watch as a thin white woman enters the village.

She walks slowly among the people, stopping to shake a hand or stroke a child's head while exchanging the Toposa greeting, "Mata!" A mother appears quickly with her sick child and presents the infant for immediate examination. Dr. Susan Nagele, Maryknoll lay missioner and family physician, is making a house call.

The child has a burning fever and, judging by the wet green leaves that cling to her body, has recently been treated with local medicine. Although Nagele has been working in this area for only a few months, most people in the village already know she is a doctor. She probes the child's distended belly and turns to an interpreter with an urgent message. "Tell her to bring the child to the clinic." Kasa, a Toposa volunteer at the clinic, is acting as translator while Nagele struggles to learn the native language. The mother asks if she and the child can ride back to the clinic in Susan's car; the walk to town is a five-hour journey. Nagele agrees. When it comes time to leave the village, the woman takes hold of Susan's arm and escorts her to the car, making sure she is not left behind.

For seven years Susan Nagele has worked in rebel-controlled southern Sudan, where a bloody civil war has been raging for decades. The fundamentalist government in Khartoum has been trying to impose strict Islamic law on the Christian ethnic tribes of the south, resulting in a struggle that has cost thousands of lives. The Sudanese People's Liberation Army (SPLA) controls most of the south and permission to enter, work, and travel in southern Sudan is closely controlled. War is a fact of life here for Sudanese and missioners alike.

Prior to coming to Narus, Nagele, forty-three, worked in a refugee camp in Nimule in another part of southern Sudan, where the war was very close. The camp was under frequent attack by government forces and after years of aerial bombings and the terror associated with the front lines, the missioner decided that she needed a change. "It was time to leave," she says matter of factly.

In the fall of 1997, Susan moved to Lotimor near the Ethiopian border and helped establish health clinics there and in the larger town of Narus. Disease, malnutrition, and an expanding population displaced by the war give Nagele and her assistants a heavy caseload.

1

1 In the middle of the day inside a typical Toposa village, women, children, and the people too old to work the fields will be the only ones to be seen.

2 A Dinka mother and child wait to see Susan Nagele at the clinic. The child was visibly upset about being in such strange surroundings.

In the war zone that is southern Sudan, machine guns and arms are everywhere. These two young Toposa boys are with their father, who carries a Russian-made AK-47.

THE HEALTH CARE FACILITY IN NARUS is housed in a new concrete building that is a short walk from the town's busy market. Looking through one of the clinic's small windows one can see groups of mud huts clustered near the front gate. A short distance beyond stand dozens of grazing cattle. Beautiful dark faces come and go into the building. They are people with strong, high cheekbones and skin the color of black onyx. They pass through the front door with purposeful strides, their impressive height and erect posture giving them a regal dignity. Once inside the clinic they proceed to wait patiently. In the Sudan, as in much of the developing world, the people are well experienced in waiting.

Inside the reception area of the Narus health care clinic, Flora Lukhumwa, a Kenyan nurse, fills out the medical history of a tall woman who sits uncomfortably in a chair while clutching her sleeping child. The v-shaped scarifications on this young mother's forehead (not to mention her six-foot height) identify her as a member of the Dinka, one of the most populous ethnic groups in the Sudan. Dozens of other patients wait their turn, sitting on simple wooden benches or on the floor. Almost all the patients are women who have some form of ritual scarring on their beautiful faces.

1

On the wall in the reception area a poster graphically reminds patients not to expect an injection at every doctor's visit. In the West, this kind of information would be intended to calm needle-phobic patients but here in the Sudan the message has a different goal. The people of southern Sudan have ancient traditions of tribal medicine and ritual scarring (for beauty) that involve a great deal of discomfort. As a result they often associate healing with some form of pain, and feel suspicious when it is omitted. One of the challenges for Susan Nagele and the other health care workers is helping their patients to find better and less harmful methods of treatment.

In a modest examining room Dr. Nagele is checking a small Dinka child, about six months old, who suffers from diarrhea. It's a common condition that is certainly uncomfortable, but the child's flooding tears tell of a larger story. Upon closer examination, Nagele discovers that the child has had crude dental work performed, probably with whatever sharp object was handy, in an effort to remove what the locals call a "false tooth"—a popular treatment for many childhood ailments from diarrhea to fever. Nagele opens the child's tiny mouth and there in the back is a deep hole with part of the jawbone exposed. Other holes attest to numerous treatments.

Unfortunately, in an attempt to alleviate the child's suffering this treatment has put the baby through a great deal of needless pain while introducing the serious risk of infection. In southern Sudan, where antibiotics are as rare as the money to buy them, infections can be life threatening. Susan turns to Joseph, her Dinka translator, with urgent instructions. "Explain to the mother that this hurts the baby, that this causes illness to the baby. Don't do this!" Nagele then turns to a visitor and says, in a tone of resignation, "Not that it will make much difference."

1 *Dr. Nagele listens closely as an elderly man describes some of his painful symptoms from a debilitating disease that has left him weak.*

2 *A Toposa Catholic stands outside the health clinic in Narus.*

2

1 *Two Toposa girls stay close to each other near the market in Narus. The older girl has already received the ritual scarring common for her tribe.*

2 *Inside the health clinic, Susan Nagele makes notes to record the condition of a Dinka woman who stands nearby. The clinic and the building itself are so alien to many tribal people that a number of door handles are broken because people are unfamiliar with how to use them.*

3 *Traditional Toposa homes are elevated to protect the occupants from animals and insects.*

1

BUT THE WORK THAT NAGELE AND THE OTHER WORKERS ARE DOING is making a great difference in the lives of the people. The nearest hospital is in Lokichoggio, Kenya, over an hour away by car on a road that is frequently attacked by snipers. It might as well be on the other side of the planet. The Narus clinic, as well as the one in Lotimor, while modestly staffed and supplied by American standards, is providing medical facilities and health education that would otherwise be unavailable to these communities. Nagele says, "Here all the patients are barefoot. The examining room is a concrete floor and the lavatory is an outhouse out back. Compared to a U.S. hospital, this is a shock. Compared to what was here before, this is a miracle."

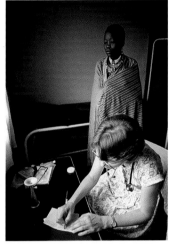

2

In addition, the delivery of medical services must hurdle a formidable language barrier in a region where so many different groups now live. During one examination, Nagele relays instructions in English to a man who translates it to Toposa to another man who finally converses in Dinka with the patient. Nagele herself is fluent in Swahili and Juba Arabic, not to mention her native English, and she is gaining facility in Toposa. She has occasion, nearly every day, to use all four languages, though these are only a few of the languages spoken here.

The introduction of modern health care in southern Sudan is awkward for the people themselves. Walking through the clinic one sees examples of a difficult transition. The handles on many of the doors of the clinic are severely bent as patients totally unaccustomed to doors in their daily lives struggle with how to use them. An elderly Toposa man, wearing a short jacket and nothing else, is being gently urged to stand on a small bathroom scale. The procedure takes over ten minutes as Flora tries in vain to communicate her directions. Repeatedly the man touches the scale with one bare foot only to pull it back, like a child sticking a toe into the ocean for the first time. At last, after much effort and a lot of giggling from the other patients gathered in the waiting room, the old man stands sheepishly on top of the white box and watches as the nurse records his weight.

3

For Nagele, her role as doctor and missioner is an expression of faith supported by a deep commitment to her Christian beliefs and a trust in the Holy Spirit. Growing up in Urbana, Illinois, in a family whose life was strongly based on Christian principles, developed in the future missioner a desire to help people in need. After graduating from Southern Illinois University School of Medicine, she immediately looked for a way to work as a doctor in the developing world, preferably within a Christian community. She found the Maryknoll Mission Association of the Faithful, and never looked back. But her work as a Maryknoller in the war zone of southern Sudan has its special difficulties. Just driving back and forth from the airport, across the border in Kenya, is a test of nerves.

SUSAN NAGELE ARRIVES AT THE AIRPORT IN LOKICHOGGIO, Kenya after the flight from Nairobi and is met by Danish relief worker Ydo Jacobs who has come to give her a lift to Narus, an hour's drive north. The road from Lokichoggio to Narus, Sudan, is a thirteen-kilometer run across an arid landscape noted for its lack of trees, its dry riverbeds, and the occasional sniper. It's a hard-packed dirt road open to the west, with a tall range of mountains guarding the eastern flank.

Ydo quickly gathers up Susan's belongings and drops them into the back of a white Toyota pickup, noting casually, "There were snipers shooting on the road yesterday and we have to convoy across." Susan climbs into the cab of the truck and asks Ydo for news of the village during her absence of a few weeks. Prior to this most recent attack, the United Nations had been providing escorts along this road but had called off the exercise once the shooting began, a fact that both Ydo and Susan note with some disappointment. A few minutes later they find the truck of Camboni Father Elia Ciapetta, who has been waiting for them north of the airport. After exchanging brisk greetings, Father Ciapetta pulls away with Ydo and Susan following close behind. They drive quickly along the road, passing rock formations and brush just big enough for someone to hide behind. The two vehicles slow down for three SPLA checkpoints where casually dressed men with AK-47 machine guns slung over their shoulders inspect them, their papers, and the truck. Allowed to proceed, they eventually reach Narus without incident.

During a quiet night sitting outside under a great sweep of glittering stars, Nagele recalled the time she was attending a patient at the camps of Nimule when she suddenly heard the distinctive sound of a Russian-built bomber flying low over the camp. Years of experience had taught her to distinguish the throaty drone of an Antonov bomber from other, less lethal planes. As she listened, the sound of the Antonov's engines changed pitch and she immediately knew that bombs were about to fall. She ordered everyone to run as fast as they could to bunkers outside the clinic. Moments after she and a handful of other health care workers huddled in the deep trench, a large bomb exploded less than a hundred yards away. "A man was trying to get his children to safety when a piece of shrapnel cut his leg off," she recalls. A number of people were killed. It was not the first time Nagele had been that close to the terror of war, but she was nonetheless terribly shaken. "War brings you down to the bottom line. When you're in a bunker and a bomber is flying over your head, you are all perfectly equal. Not much else matters," she reflects. She's aware of how living in the Sudan, with the constant threat of danger, calls for unique survival skills. "It's an abnormal situation. You have to keep things at a certain distance but the more you stay here, the more it affects your mental health." She talks about how she's had to put some of her emotions on hold in order to continue her work, fully aware that this strategy has its side effects.

By way of illustration, Nagele describes the time she was on furlough, visiting friends in Florida who happened to live near the Kennedy Space Center. "The space shuttle reentered the earth's atmosphere and I was lying in bed when the boom hit. It was like a bomb had landed and I was really shaken. It's what happens when you go back to a safe situation, you let your guard down. When I got back to Narus and big guns were going off, it didn't bother me. I had my guard up."

1

1 Ydo Jacobs, a Danish man who works for a European relief agency, drives with Susan Nagele from the airport in Lokichoggio, Kenya across the border to Narus, Sudan. Both were visibly apprehensive while they passed a section of road where rebel snipers had shot at cars the day before.

2 A group of villagers moves slowly across a field in Narus, Sudan, as they carry bags of flour donated by international relief services.

3 Along a path outside the Sudanese town of Narus, two Toposa soldiers from the Sudanese People's Liberation Army greet women coming back from drawing water from a well.

4 Automatic weapons are part of life in southern Sudan. The fundamentalist Islamic government in Khartoum has been at war with the tribes of the south for thirty years. This cattleman near Narus may also be protecting his cows from thieves.

1 *At a small Toposa village about a day's walk from Narus, a woman wears the skins, beads, and scarring that are customary for tribal women.*

2 *In Narus, Sudan, a Toposa woman, identified by the distinctive scarring pattern on her face, looks out of the window of the Catholic church.*

1

1 *Two Toposa women wait outside the medical clinic in Narus. As is the custom, women smoke tobacco from elaborate pipes.*

2 *In the town of Narus, Susan Nagele stops to talk to a group of villagers who asked about the clinic.*

3 *It took a number of hours for a cow to be butchered by machete in a field. A woman carries a large hunk of meat on her head and her child on her back.*

Some day, undoubtedly, she will return to the States, but she cannot imagine fitting in with the cultural stereotype that doctors own expensive cars and acquire wealth. Material possessions hold no interest for her. "I'm not the least bit interested in talking about expensive bathrooms," she says laughing. More important to Nagele is how she integrates her faith into her practice through compassion. "There's no training in kindness in medical school," she observes, "but it's the most important thing."

After Sunday Mass in the large church in Narus, Nagele spends time greeting people outside the main door. Her warm smiles are met with genuine affection, a sign of the bond between this doctor and the people she feels so called to accompany in their struggles, their dangers, and their faith.

3

Asmat
Assimilation

"We enrich each other by being who we are rather than trying to conform to someone else's traditions."

— *Father Vince Cole*

Vince Cole has been living among the Asmat for sixteen years and has become a cherished member of the community. When he playfully slammed his boat against a neighbor's, his prank was met with laughter.

VINCE WALKS DOWN TO THE DOCK in front of his home and begins to load his aluminum skiff with supplies: sleeping bag, mosquito netting, cooking utensils, food, water, and five-gallon jugs of gasoline and kerosene. This morning he's dressed as usual, in faded blue jean cut-offs and tee shirt, and as he ferries the equipment down, his broad feet, spread wide from years of going without shoes, slap the rough-hewn logs of the dock. He looks more like a man going on a weekend camping trip than a Maryknoll priest headed to work.

Vince Cole, a Detroit native, makes his home among the Asmat people in the small village of Sa-Er, three hours upriver from Agats, a rugged coastal town in the Indonesian province of Irian Jaya (also known as West Papua)—the western half of the island of New Guinea. His Maryknoll roots run deep; his sister is a Maryknoll nun and his brother was a Maryknoll priest. As Cole explains his vocation, "I liked the idea of mission and adventure. I never thought I'd be anywhere for more than five years." He then adds with a deep laugh, "That was sixteen years ago."

As Cole heads off toward Momogu, a village in his parish three hours further upriver, he motors through a thick haze that has engulfed the region. For weeks enormous fires have raged across Indonesia, laying an acrid blanket over much of Southeast Asia and turning the Asmat region into a dull, monochrome world. The sun has become a vague yellow disk hung behind layers of gauze while the Pomat River, normally a bright ribbon of blue winding through the emerald jungle, now cuts into the heart of Asmat like a drab road. It all belies the color, contrast, and vitality of the land.

On the river Cole passes families wedged into narrow dugout canoes. Upon recognizing the American priest, they wave a hearty greeting, some even standing up to wave hand-made paddles. Many are headed down to Erma for supplies while some are returning from the jungle after gathering sago, the staple food made from the heart of a palm that grows abundantly in the area. At one point, Cole spies a friend standing in her canoe near shore and he abruptly motors his boat in her direction. As she raises her hand in salute, Vince ignores her greeting and lets his boat slam smartly into her bow, sending her shrieking as she grabs the side of her boat before almost going over the side. A moment later she erupts in laughter and shakes her fist in mock anger. Cole, meanwhile, proceeds upriver, a devilish smile creasing his face.

Leaving the main river, Vince turns into a small tributary that runs into the tropical forest. What was before a wide boulevard is suddenly a back alley that snakes through the dense canopy as if it might be overtaken by vegetation at any moment. Cole cuts the engine and lets his boat drift silently as he sits and listens to the sounds of the jungle. Chirps, cackles, and assorted screeches mix with a constant loud buzz that arises from the forest like an exotic symphony. Vince sits back in his boat and listens. "I'm supposed to take one month off a year, but I stay in Asmat. Why would I go anywhere else? This is a vacation."

2

1 *Nine members of an Asmat family wave to Vince Cole as they make their way downriver in a dugout canoe.*

2 *Smoke from out-of-control jungle fires fill the late afternoon sky, casting a veil over the sun as three men make their way upriver in a dugout canoe.*

IN A REAL SENSE, Cole's religious life among the Asmat is marked by his assimilation into their environment. Over the last sixteen years, Vince has created a unique pastoral mission that draws heavily on Asmat culture. He has incorporated its traditions into the celebration of the Eucharist and into the very fabric of his life. In many ways his evolution as a man and a priest has been a spiritual journey that has challenged his religious ideas while expanding his role as missioner. "I found the importance of tradition here, how important it is in a person's life." He adds that the more you try to make everything the same the more you compromise the ability to reach a higher awareness.

The road that Vince Cole has chosen for his mission and his parish was not a smooth one. He recalled one of the first times he prepared to celebrate the Eucharist, dressed in his clerical stole and vestments while standing before his half-clothed congregation. "They were just staring at me with a blank look. It all had nothing to do with anything that the Asmat deal with in their daily lives." Struck by this, Cole decided to make dramatic changes in how he interacted with the people and he turned to his congregation for guidance. Together with the active participation of the community and the approval of his bishop, he introduced liturgical elements that better allow the people to celebrate Christ within the context of Asmat tradition. Soon, the church was awash in Asmat symbolism, including Cole's headdress of cockatoo feathers and his dogtooth collar.

Yet some of these changes, as necessary as they were, were difficult even for the Asmat. Because of the Asmat's powerful belief in tradition there is a corresponding fear of breaking a taboo and invoking an evil spirit. When Vince first discussed installing half a dozen "ancestral" fireplaces in the church, one of the elders lowered his head and asked, "How many people will have to die?" When the time finally came and the church was filled with smoke from the fires, Cole prayed that no one in the village fell ill. "I got down on my knees, baby. Talk about praying."

The changes that Cole and his parishioners instituted in the liturgy were part of his overall desire to celebrate Asmat culture and to help the people see themselves as worthwhile. This campaign has put Cole in conflict not only with traditionalists within the church but also with the government. For years, government educators have tried to get the Asmat to adopt modern ways and to reject their own culture, explaining these efforts as enabling them to "become human beings." In contrast, Vince Cole wants to lend credibility to the people's culture and to encourage them to deepen their connection to their own traditions. He sees the church as a way to do that. "I see Christianity as a dialogue. Becoming a Christian is just a term. Christ teaches us a lot about being human and helps us be critical of our own culture, to develop who we are. Christianity is the unifying force for the Asmat."

1

1   *It is common for Asmat men to take a direct role in the upbringing of their children.*

2   *Rufus, a catechist who works with Vince Cole, paints the Maryknoller's face in the traditional Asmat manner. As part of his effort to assimilate Asmat traditions in his liturgy, Cole wears a dog-toothed collar and headdress with cockatoo feathers while celebrating Mass.*

3   *Men from the village of Momogu take turns jumping into the Pomat River from an 18-meter-high platform built from sticks.*

The Asmat are traditional hunter-gatherers whose contact with the outside world is a relatively recent occurrence. As late as thirty years ago they were using stone tools and fifty years ago they were still eating their enemies. It has been largely through the influence of the church that the Asmat have discarded their violent past and have found peaceful alternatives to conflict resolution. But their own innocence has left them vulnerable to exploitation, primarily at the hands of large Indonesian logging companies who have employed the Asmat to harvest wood. Because the Asmat have no tradition of money, companies grossly underpay for their services while ignoring traditional Asmat values of land ownership. Cole has become involved in organizing the people, fighting for their rights, and demonstrating against the companies. He sees this as an important part of his ministry. "The Asmat need a spokesman and the church has been that for them."

3

2

The town of Sa-Er sits on an alluvial swamp where there are no roads, open fields, or playgrounds. As a result, Asmat children can often be found playing in river mud when the tide is out.

A FEW HUNDRED YARDS FROM THE MOGOMU VILLAGE, a group of men have gathered on the shore, many of them waving and calling Vince's name. They have just emerged from the jungle where they had been gathering wood. Despite the distance and lack of phones somehow these people had been anticipating Cole's arrival. Dressed in shorts and battered tee shirts, the men shout greetings to the priest as he pulls to shore. Half a dozen men jump into his boat for the short ride back to the village.

It seems that the whole village has turned out for Cole's visit; a long row of villagers follows behind him as he make his way along the boardwalk that winds among the stilt houses. He arrives at the small cabin he keeps in the village for his visits and busies himself with removing the heavy ironwood shutters, putting his bedding on the floor, and hanging his mosquito netting. His arrival represents more than a pastoral visit to the village. It's a chance for everyone to get news from the world downriver. As Vince prepares dinner on a gas stove in the back, a number of men crowd into the room and begin to fire questions at him. Cole apprises them of the progress in negotiations for a meeting between the Asmat and the logging company. Cole has aggressively campaigned for such a meeting.

1

As the men of the village listen eagerly, Vince tells them that Rufus, his catechist, has obtained copies of company records that clearly document how little the logging company has paid for the valuable wood, wood that the Asmat work so hard to bring out of the jungle. As these records may prove to be a powerful bargaining chip in the people's quest for higher pay, Vince notes that the company management is understandably upset. All the while that Cole is speaking, the men listen in rapt silence, gathered around him on the tiny porch of the cabin. The priest tells them that despite this recent positive development, the meeting is still being blocked by the representative of the Indonesian government in Erma, the town where the meeting would be held. Some heads nod in understanding as this government man is well known to be unsympathetic to the Asmat while maintaining a "cozy" relationship with the logging company.

2

The discussion goes on for several hours with a great deal of talk about what steps to take next. Cole counsels them to have faith that the existence of payment records will ultimately force the company to a meeting. The villagers seem to be in agreement and finally they leave, allowing Vince to eat his dinner of fried river fish and sago. Finally, at about ten, he turns in for the night.

3

5

1 *Villagers follow Vince Cole after he arrives in the town of Mogomu. Many of the communities that he works with are a day's journey upriver from his home. Consequently, he may visit a distant village only once a month.*

2 *The logging of exotic wood is the principal commercial industry in the Asmat area of West Papua. Indonesian companies, exploiting the people's lack of experience with money, grossly underpay families who toil for more than a day to bring a single log to the river. Vince Cole is helping the Asmat to be aware of and to petition for their rights and fair treatment by these companies.*

3 *A woman repairs a fishing net after she and a few other women spent the day catching fish in an estuary of the river.*

4 *An Asmat man proudly holds his puppy in the village of Sa-Er.*

5 *Women work a fishing net at the mouth of an estuary of the Pomat River. Fish provides much of the protein in the Asmat diet.*

4

1 In a quiet chapel that Cole built himself, the priest takes time to pray and reflect. He also made the carvings in the Asmat style that adorn the wall.

2 The Asmat are world famous for their woodcarvings, such as this shield made from ironwood.

3 Malnutrition and disease remain major problems among the Asmat, as the distended belly of this young boy illustrates.

4 A family waits patiently in the stifling heat of the jungle as the father cuts sago from a tree. Sago, a starch that is found inside a tall tree, is the principal food source for the Asmat, traditional hunter-gatherers.

The next day Vince walks through the village, stopping to look inside the church, which is only a short walk from his cabin. A simple building with a tin roof, it is clearly the largest structure in the village. Although the church is not as ornate as the one in Sa-Er, a similar series of ancestor fireplaces with their sturdy posts and platforms dominates the floor space. The "altar" is merely a raised dais. As this is an unscheduled visit, he will return in a few weeks to celebrate Mass.

His next stop is to speak with the government-appointed teacher. A number of students have complained that the teacher is abusing them, hitting them with a switch, and Vince has agreed to intervene. As Vince sits down with the teacher, a large crowd gathers around the little house. Afterward, Cole says that he listened as the teacher explained his actions, accusing the boys of misbehaving. Cole says he suggested alternative methods of discipline and asked the teacher for patience in dealing with his students, pointing out to the man that he had just arrived in the village, a full three months overdue for his assignment. Aware of the power of his words, he tried to speak firmly to the teacher but with respect, in a way that would let him save face in front of the town. "He means well," Cole says, adding that any public embarrassment might only lead to increased cruelty. Finally Cole walks to his boat for the ride back downriver, again accompanied by a throng of villagers who have collected on the riverbank to see him off.

3

4

1 Two Asmat men from Sa-Er, adorned with ochre paint and cockatoo feathers, sing songs used in traditional ceremonies.

2 Two young boys take a moment from play to greet a visitor to their village of Sa-Er.

1

COLE HAS A PROFOUND RESPECT FOR ASMAT CULTURE and acknowledges the changes that he has seen in himself through his life here. He says that the Asmat's own traditions of rebirth and spirituality made acceptance of Christian principles an easy transition, especially when framed in a context they recognize. As far as what others think of this approach, he's not concerned. "It's just what we do. If someone wants to define it, that's their prerogative. We don't worry about it." Cole is more concerned about helping the people in his parish to stand up for themselves as human beings and as Christians. He wants them to develop their independence.

His catechist Rufus underlines the importance of the priest's efforts. He credits Cole with encouraging the people to have a say in their church. "It's more of a dialog than instructions from above. We are people of God. This is not Vince's church but the people's church. So we have independence."

1

This sense of freedom is just what Vince has encouraged. But there is no doubting that the people of his village feel a strong bond between themselves and their priest. A few years ago Cole was making plans to take his periodic furlough and return to the United States. After he announced his plans to some of the villagers a delegation arrived at his door. When they asked why he was leaving Vince told them that he wanted to visit his mother. Upon hearing this, the group left, held a brief meeting, and then returned. One of the elders addressed Vince solemnly, "Okay, you can go. But you must come back."

1 *An Asmat man holds his child while walking along the boardwalk "streets" of Sa-Er.*

2 *Vince Cole, in the Asmat costume he wears for celebrating Mass, stands with some of the children of the village outside the church.*

2

Colophon

Designed by David Puelle
Typeset in Stemple Garamond and Rotis Sans Serif Light
Printed on Burgo Matt Satin 150g/m^2
Printed and bound by Milanostampa S.p.A., Italy

If you would like to hear more stories like those
in Lives of Service, we invite you to subscribe to
Maryknoll magazine, *Revista Maryknoll*, or order
The Field Afar, a 17-part video series narrated by
Steve Allen and Ken Kashiwahara.

Visit our website at www.maryknoll.org